CAMBRIDGE LIBRARY COLLECTION

Books of enduring scholarly value

Religion

For centuries, scripture and theology were the focus of prodigious amounts of scholarship and publishing, dominated in the English-speaking world by the work of Protestant Christians. Enlightenment philosophy and science, anthropology, ethnology and the colonial experience all brought new perspectives, lively debates and heated controversies to the study of religion and its role in the world, many of which continue to this day. This series explores the editing and interpretation of religious texts, the history of religious ideas and institutions, and not least the encounter between religion and science.

Life in Nature

Life in Nature, published in 1862, is a series of papers by the nineteenth-century English surgeon and popular science writer James Hinton. About a third of the material, though revised and reworked for this book, had appeared previously under the title Physiological Riddles in the Cornhill Magazine, in which Hinton explained biological phenomena for non-scientific readers. Hinton wrote this thirteen-chapter book to present a concise overview of the human body, informed by the latest scientific insights, that would be more easily intelligible for the general population than the scientific physiological data of his day. His intention was also to demonstrate the similarity between patterns occurring in the organic world and in the rest of nature. This book will be of value to historians of Victorian culture and of science as an example of how authors and publishers responded to the growing middle-class interest in scientific discoveries.

Cambridge University Press has long been a pioneer in the reissuing of out-of-print titles from its own backlist, producing digital reprints of books that are still sought after by scholars and students but could not be reprinted economically using traditional technology. The Cambridge Library Collection extends this activity to a wider range of books which are still of importance to researchers and professionals, either for the source material they contain, or as landmarks in the history of their academic discipline.

Drawing from the world-renowned collections in the Cambridge University Library, and guided by the advice of experts in each subject area, Cambridge University Press is using state-of-the-art scanning machines in its own Printing House to capture the content of each book selected for inclusion. The files are processed to give a consistently clear, crisp image, and the books finished to the high quality standard for which the Press is recognised around the world. The latest print-on-demand technology ensures that the books will remain available indefinitely, and that orders for single or multiple copies can quickly be supplied.

The Cambridge Library Collection will bring back to life books of enduring scholarly value across a wide range of disciplines in the humanities and social sciences and in science and technology.

Life in Nature

James Hinton

CAMBRIDGE
UNIVERSITY PRESS

CAMBRIDGE UNIVERSITY PRESS

Cambridge New York Melbourne Madrid Cape Town Singapore São Paolo Delhi

Published in the United States of America by Cambridge University Press, New York

www.cambridge.org
Information on this title: www.cambridge.org/9781108000703

© in this compilation Cambridge University Press 2009

This edition first published 1862
This digitally printed version 2009

ISBN 978-1-108-00070-3

LIFE IN NATURE.

LIFE IN NATURE.

BY

JAMES HINTON,

AUTHOR OF " MAN AND HIS DWELLING PLACE," ETC.

LONDON:

SMITH, ELDER AND CO., 65, CORNHILL.

M.DCCC.LXII.

CONTENTS.

CHAPTER VI.

IS LIFE UNIVERSAL?

CHAPTER VII.

THE LIVING WORLD.

CHAPTER XI.

THE ORGANIC AND THE INORGANIC.

CHAPTER XII.

THE LIFE OF MAN.

CHAPTER XIII.

Conclusion.

APPENDIX.

An Attempt towards a more extended Induction of the Laws of Life.

INTRODUCTION.

THE following pages contain a popular exposition of some of the most interesting questions which Living Bodies suggest, and are designed to present in a brief compass and easily-intelligible form a general view of them, which, it is believed, will be found more simple and more satisfactory than the ideas commonly entertained. All thoughtful persons feel that the subject of Life cannot be satisfactorily discussed on physiological grounds alone, but that it opens up some of the deepest problems which surround our existence, and raises questions the practical importance of which cannot be over-estimated. I have therefore endeavoured to give a brief expression to the views which I entertain on some of these questions ; feeling that science, happily for us, cannot, even if she would, confine herself to the mere relations of physical objects or material forces; but that she has a message for us, not less from heaven because conveyed through earthly instruments, respecting our inmost nature and our highest relations. Science, in a word, can teach us—it is her loftiest function and her greatest boon— not only respecting nature, but respecting ourselves, and so can enable us to look with purged eyes on objects which only to our blinded senses can seem trivial. We lose our privilege, we fall short of our duty, if we do not seek to gather these fruits wherever they are presented to our hand.

In perusing these pages, the reader, especially if unaccustomed to similar studies, will possibly experience more or less of a feeling as if he were losing hold of something that he could not afford to part with. He may feel that there is a tendency in them to materialize that which he cannot but regard as altogether above matter, and to reduce to the level of mechanism that which owes its chief beauty to its freedom from mechanical conditions. If so, let him by all means cherish this feeling. He could by no possibility more entirely depart from the spirit of the book than by seeking to suppress it, or in any way to diminish its force. No one more firmly or more reverently than myself believes in the authority of feelings of this character ; it is chiefly because I believe also that they can receive their perfect satisfaction only through modes of thinking such as are here set forth, that I attach any value to the thoughts. But in truth the course through which I solicit the reader to follow me is of a twofold character. I beg a relinquishment in order to a fuller possession ; a giving up as the condition of a more abundant having.

Let it be supposed that there stood before us two bodies, one a small ingot of gold, the other a mass of apparent clay ; and that a man should set about to prove to us that the small ingot was really of the same kind as the larger mass. Supposing now the former were truly gold, what would he thereby prove but that the larger mass, though seeming otherwise, was truly also gold? Yet it might seem to us, confident in our impressions, that he was taking the opposite course and trying to reduce gold to clay ; and we might for the sake of retaining the less, be impatient

of the very proofs which would establish the presence
of the more.

It is just in this way we feel when we are reluc-
tant to admit evidence which tends to demonstrate an
identity between the organic world (that is, of plants
and animals) and the rest of nature. When arguments of this kind are suspected of a tendency to
banish life from the world and interfere with the
Creator's prerogative, it is surely forgotten that those
forces and laws to which the phenomena of vitality
are thus referred, are to be judged of by their fruits,
and not to be pronounced beforehand incapable of
bearing them. To assume that we know what those
laws and forces are, and are capable of doing, is
arbitrarily to limit our own capacities. If the organic
and the inorganic worlds in nature are two presenta-
tions to us of one thing, how much more penetrating
and worthy may our knowledge become of both, each
being interpreted to us by the other!

Let it be assumed, for argument's sake, that all the
phenomena of life could be traced back to chemical
and mechanical powers, what would follow? Simply
that all the wonder and admiration with which we

now regard the living body, would be extended with increased intensity and elevation to those powers, which we call chemistry or mechanics, but which we should then perceive we had entirely under-estimated. Would it not be beautiful to see these forces stand before us thus in a new attitude and with more than doubled lustre; on the one hand confining themselves within the equable and unvarying sequence which the mechanist or chemist seems to have entirely within his grasp, and on the other breaking forth, as if to mock man's fancied rule, into the infinite variety and spontaneous grace of life?—the very union of law and liberty, reminding us that liberty is truly none the less, is only, there where law is perfectly fulfilled; that in the perfectness of freedom the perfectness of obedience lies hidden, each in each, yet in Nature separately shown to us (else undiscerning) that we may learn to know them both. But on this point it is needless to say more here, since it is discussed in other parts of the volume.

In respect to the novelty or otherwise of the views herein contained, I have no wish to make any claim to originality. I believe that in this case as in so many others, similar ideas have occurred at about the same time to various persons, showing that a new line of thought is rather an expression of prevailing tendencies than the result of individual effort. I have sought to give a reference to every writer in whom I have met with a decided similarity to my own ideas, in so far as they differ from those ordinarily received; but in case I have failed in doing this, I wish to state expressly that in publishing them under my own name, I put in no claim to be anything more than their mouthpiece. I have, however, placed at the end of the volume an essay written by me in the year 1855, and submitted at the time to some eminent scientific men, but not before published. It presents the first form in which the idea of Nutrition suggested itself to me. Of the thirteen chapters which this volume contains, four, though now revised and modified, have appeared before; they are Chapters I., II., IV., and VI.

JAMES HINTON.

London, 10th November, 1862.

LIFE IN NATURE.

CHAPTER I.

OF FUNCTION; OR, HOW WE ACT.

THE interest which attaches to the study of our bodily structure and powers is daily more widely felt, as the importance of the subject is more fully recognized, and especially as the relations which connect our bodily with our mental and moral life are better understood. Nor is this interest diminished by the difficulty with which its satisfaction is often attended. It is, indeed, stimulated rather than deadened by obstacles, and the desire to penetrate this mysterious world of material life, on which

1

all that is best and highest in humanity rests as
its foundation, is one that grows by disappoint-
ment.   For the study of life is apt to end in a
feeling of this kind.   The multiplicity of the facts
recorded by physiologists, the ingenuity of the
experiments, the intricacy of the results—the astonishing amount of light, and the insuperable darkness—produce a mingled effect upon the mind.   As
observations multiply, doubts multiply with them.
We are half disposed to ask whether we really know
anything on the subject.   Is there anything certain
in physiology at all, besides what we can see?

If there is, it must be by virtue of some fixed
and certain principles, which seem, indeed, to be
sadly wanting in this department of science.   We
appear to be, in physiological inquiries, entirely
at the mercy of our senses.   Anything might be
true, nor can we grasp any fact with a firmer hold
than mere empirical inquiry can afford.   Every inference, therefore, is open to doubt; no law is ascertained which can sustain the shock of apparent
exceptions, nor any principle established to which
we may with confidence seek to reduce anomalies.

No science has made real progress till it has passed out of this state. So long as no certain principles or necessary laws have been discovered in any branch of knowledge, we cannot tell what we may believe, and, at the best, its doctrines form a mass of truth and error inextricably mixed.

If, therefore, any relations in the vital processes could be ascertained, which must in the nature of things be true, like the propositions of geometry, or if any physiological laws could be found, based on a sufficiently wide induction to give them authority as standards, like the laws of gravitation in astronomy, or of definite proportions in chemistry, this would be a great aid both to the comprehension and to the advance of the science. And though we do not intend here to enter on any such inquiry we may try whether a clearer light cannot be thrown upon some of the points on which the main interest of physiology centres.

Too much must not be attempted at once. So, dismissing for the present all other subjects connected with the living body, we concentrate our attention on the question, Whence comes its active

power? Taking the body as it stands, supposing it
originated, developed, and nourished, by means which
we do not now consider, we ask ourselves, Can we
find the reason of its spontaneous activity?—why
action should go on within it, and force be exerted
by it on the world around?

There is a term we shall find it convenient to use
in this inquiry, and may, therefore, briefly define.
The actions of a living body are called its " functions." One of these functions is muscular motion,
whether external or internal; another is the nervous
action; and a third includes various processes of
secretion. The growth and nourishment of the body
we do not include among the " functions," as we
propose to use the term.

We inquire, then, why the living body has in
itself a power of acting, and is not like the inert
masses of merely inorganic matter? And here let
us first observe, that some other things besides the
animal body possess an active power. " It died last
night," exclaimed the Chinaman, in triumph, on
selling the first watch he had ever seen. And
certainly a watch is like an animal in some respects.

Under certain conditions, it has an active power as like that of the heart as could readily be devised, What are those conditions? They are very simple. It must contain a spring in a state of tension: that is, force must have been applied to it in such a way as to store up power, by opposing the tendency of the metal to straighten itself. Let us fix in our minds this conception of a tension, or balancing of two forces in the watch-spring. The power applied in winding it up is exerted in opposing the elasticity of the steel: it is compressed—coerced. The production of motion from it, when in this state, is a quite simple mechanical problem : let it unbend, and let wheels and levers be at hand to convey the force where it may be desired.

Let it be observed that the force thus exerted by the spring, and on which the "functions" of the watch depend, is truly the force that is applied by the hand in winding it up. That force is retained by the spring, as it were in a latent state, until it is applied to use: it exists in the spring, as tension— a state intermediate between the motion of the hand in bending it, and of the hands of the watch in their revolutions. But the motion is the same throughout. It is interrupted and stored up in the spring; it is not altered. We may say, that the tense spring is the unbent spring *plus motion*. It embodies the force we have exerted. It is not the same thing as it was in its relaxed state; it is more. And it can only pass again into the unbent state by giving out the force which has been thus put into it.

Steam is an instance of a similar thing. Water, in passing into vapour, absorbs or embodies no less than 960 degrees of heat. Vapour is not the same thing as water; it is more—it is water plus heat. Nor can it return into the state of water again, without giving out all this heat. Vapour, therefore, in respect to force, is like a bent spring, and water is like the spring relaxed.

And further, as a bent spring *tends* constantly to relax, and will relax as soon as it is permitted, or as soon as ever the force which keeps it bent is taken away, so does vapour constantly tend to return to the state of water. It seeks every opportunity, we might say, of doing so, and of giving out its force. Like the spring, it is endowed with a power of acting. Let but the temperature of the air be cooled, let a little electricity be abstracted from the atmosphere, and the force-laden vapour *relaxes* into water, and descends in grateful showers.

In the vapour, heat opposes the force of cohesion. It is not hard to recognize a tension here; the heat being stored up in the vapour, not destroyed or lost, but only latent. And when the rain descends, all this heat is given off again, though perhaps not as heat. It may be changed in form, and appear as electricity for example, but it is the same force as the heat which changed the water into vapour at the first. Only its form is changed, or can be changed.

Now the living body is like vapour in this respect, that it embodies force. It has grown, directly or indirectly, by the light and heat of the sun, or other forces, and consists not of the material elements alone, but of these elements *plus force*. Like the vapour, too, or like the spring, it constantly tends to give off this force, and to *relax* into the inorganic form. It is continually decaying; some portion or other is at every moment decomposing, and approaching the inorganic state. And this it cannot do without producing some effect, the force it gives off must operate. What should this force do then? what should be its effects? What but the "functions?"

For the force stored up in the body, like all force, may exist in various forms. Motion, as the rudest nations know, produces heat, and heat continually produces motion. There is a ceaseless round of force-mutation throughout nature, each one generating, or changing into, the other. So the force which enters the plant as heat, or light, &c., and is stored up in its tissues, making them "organic"*—this force, transferred from the plant to the animal in digestion, is given out by its muscles in their decomposition, and produces motion: or by its nerves, and constitutes the nervous force.

In this there is nothing that is not according to known laws. The animal body, so far, answers exactly to a machine such as we ourselves construct. In various mechanical structures, adapted to work in certain ways, we accumulate, or store up, force:

---

* As heat, we may say, makes water "gaseous."

we render vapour tense in the steam-engine, we raise weights in the clock, we compress the atmosphere in the air-gun; and having done this, we know that there is a source of power within them from which the desired actions will ensue. The principle is the same in the animal functions: the source of power in the body is the storing up of force.

But in what way is force stored up in the body? It is stored up by *resistance* to chemical affinity. It is a common observation, that life seems to suspend or alter the chemical laws and ordinary properties of bodies; and in one sense this is true, though false in another. Life does not suspend the chemical or any other laws; they are operative still, and evidence of their action is everywhere to be met with; but in living structures force is employed in opposing chemical affinity, so that the chemical changes which go on in them take place under peculiar conditions, and manifest, accordingly, peculiar characteristics. If I lift a heavy body, I employ my muscular force in opposing gravity, but the law of gravity is neither suspended nor altered

thereby; or if I compress an elastic body, my force
opposes elasticity, but the laws of elasticity are not
thereby altered.   In truth, the forces of gravity
and elasticity thus receive scope to operate, and
display their laws.   Just so it is in the living body.
The force of chemical affinity is opposed, and thereby
has scope to act; its laws are not altered, but they
operate under new conditions.   Owing to the opposition to chemical affinity, the living tissues ever
tend to decompose; as a weight *that has been lifted*
tends to fall.

But the living structures are not the only instances,
in nature, of bodies which tend to decompose.
There are several in the inorganic world: such
are the fulminating powders (iodide or chloride of
nitrogen, for example), which explode upon a touch.
There is a strong analogy between these and the
living tissues.   In each case, there is a tendency to
undergo chemical decomposition; in each case, this
decomposition produces an enormous amount of
force.   Explosive powders may be compared to
steam that has been heated under pressure, and
which expands with violence when the pressure is

removed. The tendencies of these bodies have been coerced by some force, which is thus latent in them, and is restored to the active state in their decomposition. This is the point of view from which the living body, in respect to its power of producing force, should be regarded. The chemical tendencies have been resisted or coerced, and are, therefore, ready, on the slightest stimulus, to come into active operation. And the " functions " are effected by this operation of chemical force upon the various adapted structures of the body. The animal is a divinely made machine, constructed, indeed, with a marvellous delicacy, perfection, and complexity; and depending upon a power, the vital modification of force, which it is wholly beyond our skill to imitate, but still involving, in the laws of its activity, no other principles than those which we every day apply, and see to regulate the entire course of nature.

We speak of " stimuli " to the vital functions— of the things which stimulate muscular contraction, or stimulate the nerves. What is the part performed by these? They are what the spark is to the explosion of gunpowder; or what the opening of the valve that permits the steam to pass into the cylinder, is to the motions of the steam-engine. They do not cause the action, but permit it. The cause of the muscular motion is the decomposition in the muscle, as the cause of the motion of the piston is the expansion of the steam; it is the relaxing of the tension. In the muscle, the chemical affinity on the one hand, and a force which we will call, provisionally, the vital force on the other, exist in equilibrium; the stimulus overthrows this equilibrium, and thus calls forth the inherent tendency to change of state. Magnets lose for a time their magnetic property by being raised to a red heat; if, therefore, to a magnet holding a weight suspended heat enough were applied, it would permit the fall of the weight. It is thus the stimulus " permits " the function.

So one of the most perplexing circumstances connected with the phenomena of life becomes less difficult to understand; namely, that the most various and even opposite agencies produce, and may be used by us to produce, the same effects upon the body. The application of cold, or heat, or friction, alike will excite respiration. Any mechanical or chemical irritation determines muscular contraction, or will occasion in the nerves of special sense their own peculiar sensations. These various agencies operate, not by their own peculiar qualities, but by disturbing an equilibrium, so that the same effect is brought about in many ways. A sudden change is the essential requisite. As almost any force will cause a delicately-balanced body to fall, so almost any change in the conditions of a living body, if it be not fatal to its life, will bring its functional activity into play. Anything that increases the power of the chemical tendencies, or diminishes the resistance to them, may have the same effect.

To recapitulate: Chemical affinity is opposed, and delicately balanced, by other force in the organic body (as we oppose forces in a machine; the elasticity of heated steam by the tenacity of iron, for example); and this affinity coming into play—spontaneously or through the effect of stimuli which disturb the equilibrium—is the secret of the animal functions. The body is not in this respect peculiar, but is conformable to all that we best know and most easily understand. The same principles are acted upon by every boy who makes a bird-trap with tiles and a few pieces of stick : here is the opposition to gravity, the equilibrium of force and resistance, and the unfortunate bird applies the stimulus.

But if the case be so simple, why has it not always been presented so ? Why has it been conceived that the living body had an inherent activity peculiar to itself? And why especially has the decomposition of the body been represented as the result, and not as the cause, of its activity ? Many circumstances have contributed to make this problem difficult of solution. In the first place, if the animal is like a machine in some respects, in others it is strikingly unlike one. All machines consist of two distinct parts : the mechanism and the power. First, men construct the boiler, the cylinder, the levers, the wheels, all the parts and members of the steam-engine, and then they add the water and the fire—first, they arrange the wheels, the balances, the adjustments of the watch, and then they bend the spring. In the body these two elements are united, and blended into one. The structure itself is the seat of the power. The very muscles, that contract, decompose; the brain and nerves themselves, in their decay, originate the nervous force. It is as if the wheels of the steam-engine were made of coal, and revolved by their own combustion;* or as if the watch-spring, as it expanded, pointed to the hour. Here is a broad distinction between all contrivances of ours and living organisms, and this made it the harder to perceive the essential correspondence. For the burning of the coal (an organic substance) to move an iron wheel, differs only in detail, and not in essence, from the decomposition of a muscle to effect its own contraction. Indeed, we are not justified in affirming, absolutely, that there is even this difference of detail. It may not be the very same portion of the muscle which decomposes and contracts; the power and the mechanism may be as truly separate in the body as in any machine of our own contriving, and only so closely brought together as to defy our

---

* The catharine-wheel is an instance of this very thing: structure and power united. But the firework is not renewed as it decomposes; the "nutrition" is wanting.

present powers of analysis. It is not unlikely that
the framework (if we may call it so) of the muscle
remains comparatively unchanged, and that fresh
portions of material are continually brought to undergo decomposition. In this way, we might perhaps
better understand the decadence of the body with
advancing age; it may be literally a wearing out.

And, secondly, the dependence of the active
powers of the body upon the decomposition of its
substance was rendered difficult to recognize, by the
order in which the facts are presented to us. Let us
conceive that, instead of having invented steam-
engines, men had met with them in nature as
objects for their investigation. What would have
been the most obvious character of these bodies?
Clearly their power of acting—of moving. This
would have become familiar as a "property" or
endowment of steam-engines, long before the part
played by the steam had been recognized; for that
would have required careful investigation, and a
knowledge of some recondite laws, mechanical,
chemical, pneumatic. Might it not, then, have
happened that motion should have been taken as a

peculiar characteristic belonging to the nature of the engine? and when, after a long time, the expansion of the steam coincident with this motion was detected, might it not have been at first regarded as consequence, and not as cause? Can we imagine persons thus studying the steam-engine backwards, and inverting the relation of the facts? If we can, then we have a representation of the course of discovery in respect to the vital functions. The animal body came before men's senses as gifted with a power of acting; this was, to their thoughts, its nature—a property of life. They grew familiar with this "property," and ceased to demand a cause or explanation of it, long before it was discovered that with every such exhibition of power there was connected a change in its composition. Only after long study, and through knowledge of many laws, was this discovery made. How then should they have done otherwise than put the effect before the cause, and say, "The animal body has an active power, and as a consequence of every exertion of that power, a part of its substance becomes decomposed?"

This is another reason why the parallel between

2

the living body and the machine has not been sooner recognized. The processes of nature are studied by us in an inverse order: we see effects before we discover causes. And such is the deadening effect of familiarity upon our minds, that the seen effect has often ceased to excite our wonder, or stimulate our demand to know a cause, before the discovery of that cause is made.

But there is yet a third reason for the difficulty that has been found in solving this problem of the nature of the animal functions. It is complicated by the co-existence, with the functional activity, of many other and different processes. The body is at the same time growing and decaying; it is nourished while it is dying. The web of life is complex to an un-paralleled degree. Well is the living frame called a microcosm; it contains in itself a representation of all the powers of nature. It cannot be paralleled by any single order of forces; it exhibits the inter-working of them all. And those processes of de-composition which generate functional activity are so mixed up with other vital processes, that no experiment can disentangle them. The relations of

the various forces can be discerned and demonstrated only by the application of known laws of
force.

Two sources of difficulty, arising from this complexity of the organic processes, may be specially
noticed. On the one hand, there are certain changes
which involve decomposition, and yet are probably
not attended with any functional activity. The
portions of the body which have given out their
force in function, may pass into still lower forms
of composition previous to their excretion as worn-
out materials: a process of decay may go on in
them, which does not manifest itself in any *external*
force. And, besides this, the decomposition which
is to bring into their orderly activity the various
structures, must itself be of an ordered and definite
character. Unregulated, or in excess, it would produce not function but disease; as, indeed, we see
in our own mechanical contrivances: not every
possible expansion of the steam, but only that which
takes place in definite direction and amount, can
raise the piston.

But, on the other hand, a still greater difficulty

in tracing the relation of decay to function, arises from the admixture, with these changes, of the opposite ones which constitute nutrition. The watch is being wound up as it goes. Perpetually giving off its force in function, this force is as perpetually renewed from the world without. And the very organs which are active by decay, are, perhaps at the same moment, being restored by nutrition to their perfect state. The disentangling of these processes may well be allowed to have challenged man's highest powers.

Let us now endeavour to apply the conception we have set forth to some of the animal functions, and see how far it is confirmed or otherwise; and, if true, to what point it carries us, and what further questions it suggests. We conceive, in the active structures of the body, a state of equilibrium very easily disturbed, existing between the chemical affinities of their elements, and a force which has opposed these affinities; and that by the operation of the stimuli which excite function, this equilibrium is overthrown.

Let us consider first the nervous system. Evi-

dently we do not take into account the phenomena
of thought, feeling, or will.   These form another
subject.   But, confining our attention to those
operations of the nervous system which are strictly
physical in their character, it may be observed, that
all the stimuli which excite them are adapted to
bring into activity the repressed chemical affinities
of the elements.   Thus the nervous force is called
into action by mechanical irritation, or motion, in
whatever form applied, by changes of temperature,
by chemical irritants, by electricity, light or sound,
and by the taste or smell of bodies.   It is hardly
possible to perceive in these various agents any property in common to which their influence on the
nervous system can with reason be referred, except
the power they all, so far as they are known to us,
possess of disturbing an unstable chemical equilibrium.   Acting upon a tissue in which the affinities
of the component elements are so delicately balanced,
and the inherent tendency to change so strong, as
in the nervous substance, it can hardly be otherwise
than that they should overthrow that balance, and
bring about a change of composition.   " In com-

pounds in which the free manifestation of chemical force has been impeded by other forces, a blow or mechanical friction, or the contact of a substance the particles of which are in a state of transformation, or any external cause whose activity is added to the stronger attraction of the elementary particles in another direction, may suffice to give the preponderance to the stronger attraction, and to alter the form and structure of the compound." *

And that a chemical change in the nervous tissue does ensue from the action of the stimulus, is proved by the fact that the same stimulus will not reproduce the effect until after the lapse of a certain interval. The necessity of time for the renewal of the irritability is evidence of an altered composition.

And may we not, in this light, form a clear and natural conception of the nervous force? A galvanic current, we know, results from chemical change in inorganic bodies. But when the nerves of any part are stimulated a chemical change is set

---

* Liebig.

up in or around them. When we touch any object, for example, the nerve-tissue undergoes such a change; the cellular substance which surrounds their terminations (Figs. 1 and 2) resembles to some degree the fulminating powders, and decomposes, though only to a limited extent, at a touch.

Fig. 1.

From the decomposition thus set up, is it not natural to believe that a peculiar force, or current, might arise, *like* the galvanic, but not the same, because the chemical changes, though resembling those which take place in inorganic substances, are not the same? The nervous force originates in a peculiar chemical change, and is, therefore, a peculiar

The nerve of the finger (after Kölliker). The smaller branches are covered with minute corpuscles. It is doubtful, however, whether these are concerned in the sense of touch.

force. But, as its source is very similar to that of galvanism, so are its characters very similar also. It is like, but different, at once in its source and nature.

Or let us take the case of hearing. In the auditory nerve, the equilibrium is so adjusted as to be
disturbed by the sonorous vibrations. An illustration

Fig 2.

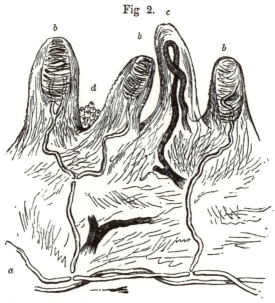

A magnified view of the termination of the nerves of the forefinger of a child
(after Wagner). *a* Nerve-trunk running on the side of the finger. *b* Termination of branch of the same within a cellular expansion, the " touch-corpuscle."
c Loop of blood-vessel. *d* Portion of the cellular tissue of the skin.

of the nature of the action is furnished by the fact
mentioned by Mr. Rogers, that masses of ice and
snow of considerable magnitude may be precipitated
from the Alpine ridges by the sound of the human
voice; the gravitation of the masses, and the resist-

ing forces which maintained them in their places,
being in such exact equilibrium that this slight
motion of the atmosphere suffices to give the preponderance to the former. Of the chamois hunters
of the Alps he says—

> From rock to rock, with giant bound,
> High on their iron poles they pass;
> Mute, lest the air, convulsed with sound,
> Rend from above a frozen mass.

This illustration, remote though it may seem, is
valuable as bringing clearly before the mind the
essential character of the process which constitutes
the animal function. For the stimulus in this case,
the aërial vibration, evidently produces the resulting
motion only by disturbing the equilibrium of the
counteracting forces.

So, too, the photographic process is a true analogue
of the physical part of vision. To prepare a plate
for photographic purposes, it is only necessary to
apply to it, in solution, chemical substances which
tend to undergo a change of composition, and the
equilibrium of which is so unstable as to be disturbed
by the rays of light. Thus prepared, the paper is

called *sensitive;*—by a blind instinct, which is often truer than studied science, for the retina, or expansion of the optic nerve within the eye, is like it. The retina consists of matter prone to change. Its elements tend to break up, and enter into new combinations. What supposition can be better warranted than that the rays of light entering the eye permit a change of composition, as they are known to do in respect to the photographic salts?

Mr. Grove by a beautiful experiment* has shown that light, falling on a plate prepared for photography, will set up a galvanic current. Does not this unavoidably suggest itself as an illustration of the process of vision? Light impinging on the retina determines therein a chemical change, which develops in the optic nerve the nervous force. This force sets up in the brain an action of the same order as that in the retina. Hence again originates a nervous force, which, conveyed back to the eye, sets up yet a third time a chemical change (in the iris), which causes the contraction of the pupil.

---

* On the Correlation of the Physical Forces.

The views recently proposed by Pflüger, in reference to the effects of electricity applied to the nerves, are strikingly in harmony with this general idea. He finds all the phenomena best explained by the conception of a tension-force and a controlling force as existing within the nerve, the balance of which the electrical agencies variously disturb.

If we pass from the nervous to the muscular system, we find abundant confirmation of our position. Of the means by which the decomposition of the muscle causes its contraction in length, and so results in motion, there is as yet no certain knowledge; but chemical action is one of the best known sources of motor force, and one of the most frequently employed. The flight of a bullet and the motion of the arm are phenomena of a similar kind. The appearances presented by muscles during contraction have been carefully observed. All muscles consist of fibres, of which 10,000 on an average would about occupy an inch. Each fibre runs the whole length of the muscle, and is connected with the tendons in which almost all muscles commence and terminate. These fibres are of two kinds, simple in the involuntary

muscles, and *striped* in those over which the will
has control. The stripes are transverse markings on
each fibre, as if it were composed of separate discs
arranged in lines (Figs. 3 and 4), and they afford a

Fig. 3.

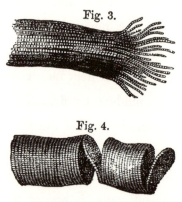

Fig. 4.

A fibre of striped, or "voluntary" muscle, showing its structure: magnified.
Fig. 3 shows the longitudinal, and Fig. 4 the transverse splitting. These and
the two following cuts are from Mr. Bowman's Paper in the *Philosophical
Transactions* for 1840.

good means of examining the process of contraction.
When a portion of fresh muscle is made to contract,
under the microscope, by pricking or otherwise irri-
tating it, the markings, or striæ, approach each other,
the muscle diminishing in length and increasing in
thickness (Fig. 5). The action is gradually propa-
gated from the point of irritation to the adjacent
parts, with a creeping motion, subsiding in one part

as it reaches another, as shown in Fig. 6, until it has traversed the whole length exposed to view. This is most probably the mode in which contraction is effected during life; and in persistent muscular

Fig. 5.

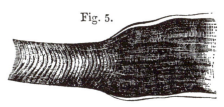

Muscular fibre partly contracted, partly uncontracted. The increase in thickness, and approximation of the striæ, mark the state of contraction.

Fig. 6.

Striated muscular fibres contracting from irritation while under the microscope. The contraction is seen travelling in waves in the direction of the length of the muscle, and affecting chiefly its upper side.

efforts it is believed that the different portions of the muscle alternately relax and contract again, and that all the fibres are not active together. The contraction of muscle is attended with a slight rustling sound, which may be heard by moving the ball of the thumb vigorously, close to the ear. In contracting, a muscle is not merely shortened; it undergoes a change which modifies its entire structure, and will bear a very much greater strain without rupture than in its uncontracted state.

The causes which determine contraction in a muscle are those which induce its decomposition. When placed beneath the microscope, it is seen to contract first at any spot where it has been broken or otherwise subjected to injury. The slightest mechanical irritation induces a local contraction, as does also the contact of air or water. In cases of lingering disease, in which the proneness to decay is increased, contraction of the muscles takes place with increased facility, and may often be excited by a touch. And the stimuli which, in health, induce action in the muscles most powerfully, are those which most strongly evoke their tendency to change of composition. Electricity, which ranks next to the nervous force as the exciter of muscular action, stands first among the physical forces as a promoter of chemical change, and is known to induce the speedier decomposition, after death, of muscles to which it has been freely applied.

But we must pass by many inviting topics, and hasten to notice one objection to the view that has been propounded, which should not be passed over, as it has probably weighed much with some minds. Certain stimulating substances, as alcohol, coffee, or tea, have been found to increase the activity, while they diminish rather than increase the waste, of the body. This question can be properly discussed only after the subject of nutrition has been passed in review; but it may be observed that there are other processes of decomposition going on in the body, besides those on which functional activity depends. It may be that these stimulants diminish that final oxidation, which precedes, more or less completely, the elimination of the waste products from the body. Or it may be, though this is not probable, that these bodies contain more force in a less amount of substance than ordinary food. Of one thing we may be confident, that no articles of diet will give us the means of creating force, or of exerting power except at the expense of the power that is embodied in our food, and so is stored up within.

And now to what end is this discussion? What advantage is gained by adopting this view of the vital functions? First, a great simplification in our idea of the living body. In respect to one of its chief characteristics, the vital organism ceases to be contrasted with the rest of nature, and becomes to us an example of universal and familiar laws. One form of force acting as a resistance to another, and so accumulating a store of power, which operates on a structure adapted to direct it to given ends;— this is the plan on which the animal creation is constructed. It is the same plan that we adopt when we seek to store up force, and direct it for our own purposes. We imitate herein the Creator; humbly, indeed, and with an infinite inferiority of wisdom and of power. But the principle is the same.

And some otherwise mysterious " properties " of living organs lose their mystery. The " contractility " of muscular fibre, and the " sensibility " of the nerves and brain, are seen to be, not mere inexplicable endowments, but names applied to the effect of their known tendency to undergo chemical change. Given the tendency to decompose, and the anatomical structure of the parts, and there must be a power to contract in muscle, and to originate the nervous in brain.

And when, in this light, we consider the *vital* force, it presents no more the same unapproachable aspect. We exonerate it from one part of the task that has been assigned to it. The vital force is not the agent in the functions; they are effects of the chemical force which the vital force has been employed in opposing. And this is the office and nature of the vital force—to oppose and hold suspended the chemical affinities within the body, that by their operation power may be exerted, and the functions be performed. When we ask, therefore, What is the vital force? we inquire for that force —whence it is derived, and how it operates—which in the organic world opposes chemical affinity. Reverting to the illustration of the watch, we have seen the functions to arise from the unbending of the spring; in the vital force we seek the agency that bends it.

This is a future task. But before we leave the subject that has occupied us now, let us take one glance at another analogy which it suggests. The actions of the body result from one form of force resisting the operation of another;—are not the revolutions of the planets regulated by the same law? Motion opposing gravity—these are the forces which (in equilibrium perpetually destroyed and perpetually renewed) determine the sweep of the orbs about the sun. Nor does observation reveal to us, nor can thought suggest, any limit to the mutual action of these kindred, but balanced powers. Life sets its stamp upon the universe; in Nature the loftiest claims kindred with the lowest; and the bond which ties all in one Brotherhood, proclaims one Author.

CHAPTER II.

OF NUTRITION; OR, WHY WE GROW.

WE are continually dying. In all our actions force is given off, the very same force by which the body lives; and portions of our frame, accordingly, waste and are cast off. This process implies an opposite one. The life, constantly ceasing, is constantly renewed. Throughout the adult state nutrition proceeds *pari passu* with decay; in youth it is in excess, and results in growth; in age, the preponderance of the decay predicts the end. But new life springs from the old, and in its offspring the perishing organism repeats and multiplies its youth. How is this marvel wrought? By what agency does the perpetually failing life renew itself, and rise up fresh and vigorous from its ceaseless struggle with decay?

3—2

It is a wonderful thing—Life, ever growing old, yet ever young; ever dying, ever being born; cut down and destroyed by accident, by violence, by pestilence, by famine, preying remorselessly and insatiably upon itself, yet multiplying and extending still, and filling every spot of earth on which it once obtains a footing; so delicate, so feeble, so dependent upon fostering circumstances and the kindly care of nature, yet so invincible; endowed as if with supernatural powers, like spirits of the air, which yield to every touch and seem to elude our force; subsisting by means impalpable to our grosser sense, yet wielding powers which the mightiest agencies obey. Weakest, and strongest, of the things that God has made, Life is the heir of Death, and yet his conqueror. Victim at once and victor. All living things succumb to Death's assault; Life smiles at his impotence, and makes the grave her cradle.

Truly it seems as if there were something here not only mysterious and wonderful (for that everything in Nature is), but peculiar and unlike all beside. It seems as if a power had its seat in living things, which could maintain and extend itself by some inherent faculty, could subdue by a spontaneous operation surrounding forces, and hold in subjugation all that tended to its injury.   And for a long while this view was entertained.   It is natural; and until an extensive knowledge of the physical laws had been attained, it seemed to be necessary.   All have heard of the Vital Principle.   This was the agent supposed to reside in living things, and (either with conscious design or unconsciously) to build up, model, maintain, and use the organic frame.

This figment, however, has long been overthrown. The labours of physiologists (among which those of Dr. Carpenter hold an eminent place: see especially his paper on the Correlation of the Physical and Vital Forces in the *Philosophical Transactions* for 1850) have revealed the proofs of a profounder harmony in Nature.   Life is strong, because it is dependent; immortal, because it draws its being from a perennial source.   All things minister to it.   The tender organic frame needs no self-preserving power within, because all the natural powers are its servants.   The earth and air and distant orbs of heaven feed it with ceaseless care, and supply, with unfailing constancy, its wants. Life is in league with universal forces, and subsists by universal law.

For the growth and nourishment of organic bodies may be seen to result from well-known agencies, and to be in conformity with common and all-pervading laws. But, first, it is needful to limit our inquiries, and to mark out distinctly the question to be considered. The fable of the fagot of sticks which were easily broken one by one, but resisted all efforts when tied together, is peculiarly applicable to the study of Life, though its moral needs to be read the other way. We must divide to conquer. We have discussed the active powers or " functions " of the body, and have seen them to result from chemical changes within it, by which (as by the relaxation of a tense spring) force is set free, and the characteristic actions of the various organs ensue. In living bodies chemical affinity has been opposed, so that they represent forces in a state of tension; their elements are arranged in a manner from which chemical affinity tends to draw them. The question we now propose is—By what means is this arrangement of the elements effected? The actions of the body, produced

by chemical change within it (its partial and regulated decomposition), have been compared to the
motions of a clock, produced by the regulated gravitation of its weights. The present question, therefore, would be, How are the weights raised?

It is evident that this question does not cover all
the ground that remains. It leaves on one side at
least two distinct subjects—one the first origination
of Life; the other, the FORMS which organic bodies
assume. Neither of these questions comes within
our present regard. Our inquiry is, how living
organisms grow and are nourished under existing
conditions; and that only in one aspect of the case.
For the body not only increases in size and weight
from its first formation till maturity, but while this
process is going on it receives a certain shape. It is
not only *nourished* but *organized*. The various parts
are fitted to each other, and the whole presents, in
every order of creatures, a typical or specific form,
which is, indeed, one of the chief distinctions of the
organic world. But we do not here concern ourselves with this curious fact. We ask only, by what
means new materials are added to the living body in

its earlier stages, and waste is repaired when it has attained its perfect stature? How these materials are shaped into characteristic forms is a future question. We will take our fagot stick by stick.

To make clear our meaning, let us suppose ourselves looking at a portion of the white of an egg—albumen, as it is called. This has no power of performing actions; it has no defined shape; it is contained in the shell as it might be in any other vessel; it has not even any structure, such as fibres or cells, which the microscope reveals; it is simply a viscous fluid. Yet it is an organic substance. Life is in it. It is, indeed, the basis of all animal structures, and the great source from which they are formed and nourished. That which constitutes it living is the mode in which its elements are arranged. It consists mainly of three gases (hydrogen, oxygen, and nitrogen), and one solid (carbon), with small quantities of other bodies, of which the chief are sulphur, phosphorus, and lime. But these elements are not arranged according to their ordinary affinities. Exposed to the air, albumen decays; the carbon unites with oxygen and forms water, and with nitrogen to form ammonia. Similarly, the sulphur and phosphorus select some other ingredients of the albumen, or of the atmosphere, to unite with them into simpler compounds. In time, the process is complete, and from being an organic substance the albumen has wholly passed into a variety of inorganic substances. In doing so, it has given out a certain amount of force, chiefly in the form of heat (the temperature of decaying bodies is well known to be above that of the surrounding air); and this force, if the albumen had formed part of a muscle or a nerve, would have been operative in the function of the same. Now it is on account of this force, which is in the albumen, and is not in the inorganic substances which are formed by its decay, that it is called organic. It could not be albumen without some force having made it so. Hydrogen, and nitrogen, and carbon, and oxygen would no more form albumen (against their tendency to form carbonic acid and water and ammonia), without some force compelling them, than a stone would poise itself in the air (against its tendency to fall to the ground), without some force compelling it.

We seek, then, the source and laws of the force by which the elements of the living body are placed in these relations to each other, and instead of forming the ordinary chemical compounds, are formed into organic substances. And here we turn to facts. Every one knows that decaying substances are the seats of life. The "mould" that infests the stores of thriftless housekeepers, and the fungi that grow on damp and rotting wood, are instances. These low forms of vegetation live on the decaying matter. Let us consider what takes place in their growth. On the one hand, the wood or other substance, in its decay, is giving out force; on the other, the developing plants are acted upon by force, and are embodying it in their structure. One body is ceasing to be organic, and therein is giving off its force, and in immediate connection with it another body is becoming organic, and therefore is receiving force into itself. Can we be misinterpreting these facts in saying that the former process is the cause of the latter; and that the decay gives out the force which produces the growth?

To take an illustration. Conceive two watch-springs, one bent, the other relaxed (and the former somewhat the more powerful), so connected together that the unbending of the one should cause the bending of the other.   The bent state, here, would be transferred from the one spring to the other ; the one would cease to be bent as the other became bent. But we have seen that the organic state of matter may be compared to the bent state of a spring; that it also is an embodying of force.   Is it not quite as simple, then, that the "organic state" should be transferred from the decaying body to the growing one ?   It is, in each case, simply a transference of force from the one to the other; of the presence of which force the organic state, like the mechanical tension, is the effect and sign.   Thus, in the case of plants growing on decaying substances, the decomposing process in their food becomes an organizing process in them; the force arising from the decomposition becomes, and is, their "vital force."

Let us trace the process again; the wood, as an organic substance, contains vital force; as it decays, it passes into inorganic substances (such as carbonic acid, &c.) in which there is no vital force.

During this decay, therefore, the vital force that was in the wood has passed forth from it. What has become of it? Part of it has been given out as heat; but part of it, evidently, has been, as it were, transferred to the fungus which has grown at its expense. The wood *was* living, the fungus lives now; the wood has decayed, the fungus has grown ; the wood, in its decay, has given out force; the fungus, in its growth, has taken up and embodied force, and is ready in *its* decay to give it off again. The life of the wood has, in short, been transferred to the fungus. The force has changed its form, but it is the same force in both.

The fungus could not have grown if the wood had not decayed, the force would have been wanting; as in the action of a balance, one scale cannot rise unless the other falls. The living state is, in respect to the force of chemical affinity, as the raised state is in respect to the force of gravity. When one scale of a balance falls, the " raised state " is transferred from it to the other scale ; so, when one organic body decays and another grows upon it, the " living state " is transferred from the decaying to the growing body.

It is transferred to the one, while it ceases, and because it ceases, in the other.

In this instance the law of growth is presented to us. Matter is rendered organic, either through the decomposition of other organic matter, or through the medium of chemical processes which resemble that decomposition in giving out force. The nutrition of living bodies is, in brief, an illustration of the axiom that action and re-action are equal and opposite.

This is easily perceived if the conception of the organic state as involving an opposition to chemical affinity is kept before the mind. The decomposition of one portion of organic matter may cause other matter to become organic, as the fall of one portion of matter may cause another portion to rise. The downward movement generates force, the upward absorbs it; the fallen body represents the inorganic, the raised body the organic state. Or it is as the downward motion of a pendulum develops the force from which its upward movement results; or as a heated body contracts while it cools, and causes expansion in the things around. But in truth, the possible illustrations are innumerable, for a

process essentially the same is presented to us continually in nature under every variety of form:—a
change of one kind producing its opposite. It is this
to which (in its mechanical form) the name of *Vibration* has been applied; as when a tense string that
has been deflected from the straight line is let go, its
motion towards the central line reproduces the deflection; the one motion producing the force, which the
other, as it were, uses, or absorbs.

The vital force, from carbonic acid, water, and
ammonia, produces albumen; chemical force from
albumen produces carbonic acid, water, and ammonia. These two processes are not only different,
they are strictly opposite to each other, and because
they are opposite, they are so closely interlinked.
The opposition of life to chemistry is the secret of
its source. Life is an action produced by its
opposite. It has its root in death, and is nourished
by decay.

The first suggestion of this view, as I have
recently become aware, appears to have been made
by Dr. Freke, of Dublin, who, in a work "On
Organization," published in 1848, endeavoured to

show that for the origination or formation of one
organic body, there is a necessity for a simultaneous
disorganization or decay of another; so that in all
life both these processes are in operation together.
His words are : " Thus are two essentially distinct
and opposite processes concerned in producing the
phenomena of active life ; are of necessity in operation for the production of what we imply when
we say of a thing ' it lives ; ' and thus, too, it becomes
apparent how death is essentially a part of life."
Again, in some papers published in 1852, Dr. Freke
says, in discussing the nature of the vitalizing process : " We find that what one was obtaining, the
other was losing ; at the same time that the elevation
of dead matter to the organized condition was in
progress, another and directly opposite process was
taking place: namely, the body which was con-
ferring that organization was itself undergoing the
process of disorganization ; was itself descending in
the scale of life."

Dr. Henry, also, of the Smithsonian Institute at
Washington, has advocated the same doctrine.   In
a Report on Agriculture, published in 1857, he thus

speaks, illustrating the general question by the growth of a potato: " If we examine the condition of the potato which was buried in the earth, we shall find remaining of it (after it has given origin to a young plant) nothing but the skin, which will probably contain a portion of water. What has become of the starch and other matter which originally filled this large sac? If we examine the soil which surrounded the potato, we do not find that the starch has been absorbed by it; and the answer which will naturally be suggested, is that it has been transformed into the material of the new plant, and it was for this purpose originally stored away. But this, though in part correct, is not the whole truth; for if we weigh a potato prior to germination, and weigh the young plant afterwards, we shall find that the organic matter contained in the latter is but a fraction of that which was originally contained in the former. We can account in this way for the disappearance of a part of the contents of the sac, which has evidently formed the pabulum of the young plant; but here we may stop to ask another question, By what power was

the young plant built up of the molecules of starch?
. . . . The portion of the starch, &c. of the
tuber, as yet unaccounted for, has run down into
inorganic matter, or has entered again into combi-
nation with the oxygen of the air, and in this
running down, and union with the oxygen, has
evolved the power necessary to the organization
of the new plant."

A similar view has been argued by Professor
Le Conte, of the South Carolina College, Columbia.*
"It is well known that in the animal body there
are going on constantly two distinct and apparently
opposite processes, viz. decomposition and recomposition of the tissues; and that the energy of life
is exactly in proportion to the rapidity of these
processes. Now, according to the ordinary view,
the animal body must be looked upon as the scene
of continual strife between antagonistic forces,
chemical and vital; the former constantly tearing
down and destroying, the latter as constantly building up and repairing the breach. In this unnatural

---

* See the *American Journal of Physical Science*, November,
1859 ; or the *Philosophical Magazine*, February, 1860.

warfare the chemical forces are constantly victorious, so that the vital forces are driven to the necessity of contenting themselves with the simple work of reparation. As cell after cell is destroyed by chemical forces, others are put in their place by vital forces, until finally the vital forces give up the unequal contest, and death is the result. I do not know if this view is held by the scientific minds of the present day as a fact, but it certainly is generally regarded as the most convenient method of representing all the phenomena of animal life, and, as such, has passed into the best literature of the age. Certain it is, however, that the usual belief, even among the best physiologists, is that the animal tissue is in a state of unstable equilibrium; that constant decomposition is the result of this instability, and that this decomposition, and this alone, creates the necessity of recomposition — in other words, creates the necessity of food. But according to the view which I now propose, decomposition is necessary to develop the force by which organization of food or nutrition is effected, and by which the various purely animal functions of the body are carried on: that decomposition not only creates the necessity, but at the same time furnishes the force of recomposition."

The phenomena of fermentation afford a test of the soundness of this conception. Vegetable juices during fermentation undergo a process of slow decomposition. If, during this process, certain peculiar germs are present, a plant consisting of cells, and low in the scale of vegetable life, is developed. This plant is what we call the Yeast. Now, if the force given out by the liquid in fermenting be the cause of the growth of the plant, yeast should never be formed unless fermentation is going on. If, on the other hand, the growth of the plant be (as has been supposed by some) the cause of the decomposition, then fermentation should never occur unless that growth takes place. But it is well known that the yeast plant is never developed except during fermentation, while fermentation will take place, although more slowly, without any formation of yeast. It follows, therefore, that the growth depends upon the decomposition, and not the decomposition upon the growth.

4—2

But fermentation is excited by the addition of yeast, and proceeds more successfully in proportion to the rapidity with which the yeast cells are developed. Why should this be if the formation of the living cells is only the effect, and not the cause, of fermentation?

The intimate connection of growth and decay explains this fact. The yeast excites fermentation because it is itself exceedingly prone to decompose; more prone than the liquid to which it is added. And in decomposing it communicates the impulse of its own change to the matter around it, so disturbing the equilibrium of the elements, and bringing about, in a few hours, chemical changes that would otherwise have occupied a much longer time. And this more active decomposition in the fermenting fluid reacts again upon the cells of the yeast, and produces in them a rapid growth and multiplication. They afford the outlet, as it were, for the force given out by the chemical changes to which they have furnished the stimulus.

In thus inducing a more vigorous growth by instituting, primarily, a more energetic decay, the

effect of the yeast-plant is analogous to many processes in the animal body. For example, there is
reason to believe that the limbs are powerfully
developed by exercise, and that muscles waste if not
kept in use. But the action of a muscle depends
upon an energetic decomposition in it, and in this
more energetic decomposition of the active than of
the inactive muscle, we may easily recognize the
cause of its greater vital development. The stimuli
which call it into functional activity produce chemical
changes in it, as the yeast does in fermentable
liquids; and the larger growth consequent thereon
is like the more abundant development of the yeast
cells in actively fermenting fluids.

This effect may be illustrated mechanically. The
pendulum rises by the force of its fall, and will be
made to rise the higher by any impulse which makes
its fall more rapid. This aspect of the subject is
further illustrated in the Appendix.

Recognizing this dependence of nutrition on decay,
we have in our hands a clue which will guide us
through the labyrinth of the vital phenomena. For
the most striking, and at the first view the most

marvellous aspect of life, is the coexistence and inseparable interlinking, in every part and process, of these opposites. Building up and pulling down, formation and destruction, results of chemical force and results opposed to chemical force, are ever going on together. Till the one class of operations is seen to be a consequence of the other, an air of impenetrable mystery rests over all. But if this relation is recognized, the entire cycle of physical life presents itself to us under a new aspect; and the problem of vitality, though peculiar in its details, and of almost infinite complexity, is seen to belong essentially to a class of problems already solved.

Water regaining its level, and rising, as in an enclosed circuit it will do, by virtue of its fall, presents to us in a simple form the very same relations of force. "You see," says Bishop Berkeley, at the conclusion of his celebrated *Dialogues on Matter*, "the water of yonder fountain, how it is forced upwards in a round column to a certain height, at which it breaks and falls back into the basin from whence it rose; its ascent as well as descent proceeding from the same uniform law or principle of gravitation." May not a fountain, indeed, picture to us the relations of the forces in the organic body? How mysterious a fountain would be to an observer unacquainted with the law that water will find its level, and that a gravitating motion may produce a motion opposed to gravity! How like its continued upward and downward flow, with its hidden source, is to the intermingled processes of life; two opposites bound up in one, and presenting to us the effects of a single cause! For chemical force is to the organic body as gravity is to the fountain, the source of all its actions, opposite though they are.

In a fountain the operation of gravity is regulated, and directed in a certain way, so as to produce, in the elevation of the water, an effect directly opposed to its own primary action; in life, the operation of chemical force is regulated and directed in certain ways, so as to produce, in nutrition, results directly opposed to its primary action. Thus chemical affinity, at the same time, produces and destroys the living frame, as gravity at the same

time produces and destroys the fountain. There is
a constant flux maintained by a hidden power: a
mystery, necessarily, until the more mysterious
simplicity and grandeur of the LAW are known.

We must take a larger view than we are naturally
apt to take of the vital relations, and extend our
thoughts to embrace processes which do not present
themselves immediately to our sense. There is in
organic life, truly, a threefold process: the first link
of which is a chemical operation external to the
living frame itself, a part of the general force of
nature, of which the vital force is a particular form
and modification only. In the apparent aspect of
living things, this primary operation is concealed
from sight, and so it is naturally overlooked; as in
a fountain the uninstructed eye takes no account of
the previous elevation and fall of the water. Life
seems to begin with the nutrition—an action opposed
to chemical force; but we look farther back, and
recognize a precedent chemical change as the originating power. In respect to force, the chain is
this: first, in the world around, an action due to
chemical force; then, resulting from this, a change

opposed to chemical force, which is the nutrition of the living body; then again a chemical .change, which is its function or decay. So in the fountain there is, first, the gravitating motion of the water, then the upward motion due thereto; and then again a gravitating motion.

And thus, too, we may discern in what the special characteristic of the vital process consists. It does not lie in the forces at work, nor in the laws according to which they operate. Physical life is a result of the natural laws, and not an exception to them; but the conditions are peculiar. As in a fountain the force of gravity, so in a living body the force of chemical affinity, receives a particular direction; and instead of producing heat, or electricity, or motion, as it does in the inorganic world, it is made to produce a force which directly opposes its own effects. This special direction of the effect of chemical force is the peculiarity of life.

But why the peculiar substances which constitute organic bodies should be formed ;—why the chemical force, thus acting, should produce the albumen, fibrine, and gelatine, of which animals chiefly con-

sist, or the woody fibre which makes up the mass
of vegetable structures ;—is a separate question, and
one on which at present much darkness rests. Not
that it is a *peculiar* mystery. The formation of
water from hydrogen and oxygen, or of chalk from
carbon, oxygen, hydrogen, and lime, in obedience
to their chemical affinities, is no more understood
than the formation of albumen from these and other
elements in opposition to the affinities which draw
them another way. When the chemist has told us
why two gases, chemically united, should form
water, he may ask the physiologist with a good
grace why four or five gases and solids, vitally
united, should form albumen. These two facts rest
on the same basis. The relation of what the chemist
calls " elements " to the substances formed by their
union, is one on which science is yet almost wholly
silent. Meanwhile the relations of the forces concerned are capable of a separate demonstration, and
we need not delay, until we know why albumen or
fibrine should be formed, our inquiry into the laws
displayed in their formation.

CHAPTER III.

OF NUTRITION.—THE VITAL FORCE.

THUS we have clearly before us the idea of the organic state as one of *tension*, dependent upon an opposition to chemical affinities. And we see, too, how this tension is produced, at least in some cases : namely, by the previous operation of those very affinities themselves. But some interesting questions suggest themselves here, to which it is in our power to give at least probable answers. We may ask whether this dependence of the living state on chemical action is universal; or whether other forces, such as light and heat, may not also directly produce it? There appears reason to believe that the latter is not the case; but that a process of chemical change is always connected with the vitalizing of matter, and that any other forces

which contribute to this end do so by first exciting
chemical activity.　Where the latter is not present,
no amount of other force suffices to induce the vitalizing process.　And so far from these other forces
being always absorbed when growth is in progress,
we see a notable instance of the contrary in the germination of the seed, which is attended with a decided
rise of temperature.　It appears that here the amount
of chemical change is in excess of the vital action
consequent upon it, and that, therefore, while a part
of the force it generates goes to reproduce the vital
state, and bring about the growth of the young plant,
part of it passes off as heat.　So too, in some of the
functions of the animal (muscular motion, for example), the decomposition of the tissues seems to
generate more force than the function consumes, and
the temperature rises.

The part played by the various other forces which
are known to contribute to the process of vitalization
(of which heat and light are the chief) would seem,
therefore, to be either that of furnishing the conditions for chemical action, or of adding to its intensity.
In both these ways their influence is essential.　The

effect of a moderately high temperature in facilitating chemical changes is well known, and its influence upon life can be perfectly understood upon that ground. Each tribe of living creatures seems to have a range of temperature within which its vital processes can be most perfectly carried on; as we see in the hybernation of some warm-blooded animals during winter; and the similar state of inactivity to which warmth reduces certain of the reptile class. On vegetable life the influence of heat is so predominant, that Boussingault has made it the basis of calculation, and states that the same annual plant, in going through its complete development in different climates, receives on the whole the same amount of solar light and heat, its time of growth being shorter or longer, in strict proportion to their greater or less amount.

But further: in order to see fully the relation of chemical action to the production of the vital state, it is necessary to have recourse to the conception of a resistance or limitation to it. A natural action, such as the fall of a heavy body, as we have seen, may bring about a condition opposite to itself; it is the law

of vibration: but in order that it may do so that action
must take place under resistance, or must be incomplete. The pendulum rises from the effect of its fall,
because that fall is partial, and fails of reaching the
attracting body. If it fall to the earth, though the law
of its action and the total amount of the effect produced are the same, yet the practical result is different. Other forces, such as heat and sound, are
produced, but the raised condition of the falling body
does not re-appear. It is the same with the vibrations of a string; the tension which is necessary
before vibration can be induced in it seems to intro-
duce a resistance to the full recoil of the particles
upon each other, so that their partial return after
being drawn aside carries them again asunder. Now
a similar thought respecting the chemical action
which is the cause of growth, seems to be appropriate
to, and demanded by, the facts. Living matter appears to afford such a limitation to chemical change,
when taking place in relation with it, and so it
educes a vitalizing action from that change. It
gives this direction to the force generated by decomposition, or by other processes of chemical union, by

holding them as it were in partial check, and causing the chemical tendencies to fall short of their full satisfaction. Nor is the power of limiting the chemical processes on the part of organic bodies a mere supposition: it is a power which they are known to possess, which is indeed one of their most obvious and familiar properties. Living bodies are distinguished by their resisting to some extent the operation of chemical forces; and to this resistance their power of causing chemical change to produce living matter may be referred. When the forces are too great, and overcome the resistance, then there results from them only decomposition. They run on to the destruction of the organic state, and the dissipation (in heat or other inorganic forms) of the force that it embodied.

It thus appears that the origination of organic Life in Nature remains an open question. Our knowledge extends at present only to its reproduction and increase. To these there is a sufficient key in well-known laws; and they may be carried to any extent without demanding the supposition of other than familiar agencies and established principles. But the question of the first arising of the living state, the primary direction of the chemical or other force to produce an organic arrangement of the elements, remains as yet undecided. There is no difficulty in conceiving such a modification of chemical action to arise in accordance with the natural laws; and that there should be forces existing which must operate, under given circumstances, to determine the organic arrangement of elements when it does not exist before. Indeed, M. Berthelot's magnificent experiments, in which some of the simpler organic substances have been formed from their elements by the application of force in the laboratory, seem to exhibit this very fact before our eyes.* And the differences pointed out by Professor Graham† between the two great divisions of matter (the crystalline, and the colloidal or gelatinous) have a most suggestive bearing in the same direction. He remarks respecting the latter (or colloidal) substances, that they contain

---

* *La Chimie Organique fondée sur la Synthèse.* Par M. Marcellus Berthelot.

† " On Liquid Diffusion as applied to Analysis." *Philosophical Transactions,* 1861. Gum, or starch, or isinglass, may be taken as examples of colloidal substances.

force; "the probable primary source of the force appearing in the phenomena of vitality." He shows, too, that there are many other forms of this kind of matter besides the organic: the hydrated silicic acid, for example, from which in geologic periods flint appears to have been formed. He compares these substances to water kept from freezing at a temperature below 32°, or to a saline solution more than saturated with the salt, and ready to crystallize on the slightest shock ;—a condition of tension essentially the same as that which is the great distinction of the organic substance. But still we do not know what way the organic state of matter may have arisen in nature. We are equally in the dark, indeed, as to the origination of any of the other forces or arrangements of elements; and the entire body of our knowledge must be advanced before we can satisfactorily discuss it. The difficulty is increased by the absolutely contradictory results, hitherto, of the experiments made by different observers to ascertain whether organized bodies arise in infusions of vegetable matter, without the presence of germs from which they may be developed. Each

5

man will probably entertain his own opinion. My own is, that both organic matter, and organized creatures did probably, and possibly may still, arise in the ordinary course of nature. And I am confirmed in this opinion by the emphatic language (three times repeated) of Genesis: " And God said, Let the earth bring forth grass, the herb yielding seed, and the fruit tree yielding fruit after his kind, whose seed is in itself upon the earth : and it was so. And the earth brought forth grass, and herb yielding seed after his kind, and the tree yielding fruit, whose seed was in itself after his kind." And again: " And God said, Let the waters bring forth abundantly the moving creature that hath life, and fowl that may fly above the earth, in the open firmament of heaven. And God created great whales and every living creature that moveth, which the waters brought forth abundantly after their kind." And again: " And God said, Let the earth bring forth the living creature after his kind, cattle and creeping thing and beast of the earth after his kind; and it was so."*

* Genesis i., verses 11, 12, 20, 21, 24.

It is indeed remarkable that in the teeth of these words the religious sentiments of men should have been roused against the opinion that the earth and the waters brought forth, or might be supposed probably to have brought forth, living creatures. And more especially does this appear strange when we find that the natural and obvious meaning of the words is still further established to be in favour of what has been called " spontaneous generation," by the arguments founded on them by some of the Christian Fathers: Saint Augustine urging, on this very ground, that the assembling of the animals in the ark must have been for the sake of prefiguring the gathering of all nations into the Church, and not in order to secure the replenishing of the world with life.*

That there is nothing which ought to excite distrust in the view of the, so called, spontaneous origin of living creatures may be further confirmed by a curious passage which occurs in Bacon's *Atlantis,* and which, irrational though it doubtless is, shows in

---

* Quoted in the first volume of *Cosmos.*

which direction his judgment tended. " We make a number of kinds of serpents, worms, flies, fishes, of putrefaction, whereof some are advanced (in effect) to be perfect creatures, like beasts or birds. . . . Neither do we this by chance, but we know beforehand of what matter and commixture, what kinds of those creatures will arise."

We dismiss, however, as premature, any discussion of the origin of organic life, or consequently of the vital force. But we perceive that from our present point of view the vital force exists simply in a peculiar arrangement of elements, involving a tension of a special kind. By whatsoever means this arrangement may be produced, the force thus embodied in it is equally called vital. The characters of the force are due to that arrangement; they flow from it rather than are concerned in its production : just as in the case of the other forces, such as heat or electricity, the peculiar properties they manifest are the results and not the causes of the states of matter in which they consist.

The vital force, then, is like the other forces in nature in this, that it causes, or exists in, a state of

tension; it is peculiar in respect to the characters of
the tension in which it is exhibited. One of these
characters is so striking and universal as to deserve
especial mention. An almost constant process in the
rendering inorganic matter organic is the giving off
of oxygen; as constant, in the return to the inorganic state, is its absorption. The whole process
may be said to constitute a great de-oxidation and
re-oxidation: the de-oxidation produced by force and
constituting a tension, the re-oxidation a return, a
rebound as it were, to the former state, reproducing
the force. And on the constant supply of oxygen all
functional power, and therewith the continuance of
the life, depends. The living body and the atmosphere around it constitute an inseparable whole.
The once united elements still retain, in reality, their
coherence—put asunder by force, and for temporary
purposes, but pledged as it were to a deeper and inviola-
ble union. In the re-uniting of the parted elements
is effected the end and object of the whole process,
the functions of animal life. Complex, wonderful,
and beautiful as it is, surely the wonder and beauty
of the organic world rise in this view to a yet greater

height. For in the de-oxidation and re-oxidation of the hydrogen in a single drop of water, we have before us, truly, so far as force is concerned, an epitome of the whole of life.

Thus, too, it appears that the production of the organic state is a true chemical analysis. In endeavouring to appreciate it, we must not limit our attention to the organic substances themselves; we must comprehend in our view also the liberated oxygen; otherwise we receive a false impression. Between all organic bodies and the oxygen around, a tension exists, which is of the essence of their being. By any one with a competent knowledge of unchangeable relations it might have been foretold, seeing the nutrition achieved by the plant, that the animal must breathe. The vital air does but give us back our own;—our own, though by the lack of it we live.

And thus we need not, as indeed we cannot rightly, regard the organic substances as maintained by an affinity among their elements. For these substances have an onward and outward look; they imply a reference to something apart from themselves. The imprisoned gases pine for their wonted partner, and stretch themselves out towards their destined liberator. Set free from constraint their affinities operate again, and the materials of the living body and the atmosphere re-unite themselves. But no "affinity" need be supposed to hold together the organic substances; their elements are coerced into union by extraneous force, not drawn to it by attraction from within. In this respect these substances are like the inorganic compounds in which force is embodied, such as gunpowder, in which the components are placed side by side in definite proportions, but are not united to each other. The organic substance is analogous rather to the mixed gases of oxygen and hydrogen, resulting from the decomposition of water, and ready to explode on the application of an electric spark, than to a compound united by affinity.

But in considering the source of the force contained in organic bodies, we must not forget the frequent presence in them—the constant presence in all their most active portions—of nitrogen, solidified as it were from that gaseous condition to which it has a constant tendency to return. The presence of this same element, in the like solidified form, characterizes also the explosive compounds; gun-cotton, for example, being formed by saturating the fibre with nitrogen. It is hardly to be doubted that one great element in the tendency of living structures to decompose, and to exert force, consists in the tendency of the nitrogen to escape from the bondage in which it is thus placed. And so a part of the activity of the body would be due to the coercion, not of the chemical but of the mechanical properties of its constituents, by the union into which they have been forced.

For an example of the application of the idea of Life, as a twofold operation of one force, to the details of animal existence, we may refer to the development of the caterpillar into the moth, which is generally accompanied (as in the case of the silkworm) with a special activity of secretion. The silk is produced through a decomposing process; it is less living than the blood or tissues from which it is derived. Part of the force that was embodied in these has been given off; one portion of the creature's substance has sunk lower. May we not well believe that the remaining portion, through that sinking, has risen higher? To this very secretion we may trace the force by which the vital condition of the insect is elevated to a correspondence with the demands of the higher organization it is destined to assume. By the operation of this simple law, the creature itself is furnished with protection and warmth, and fitted for its new life, while man's activities are evoked and his pleasures multiplied.

And looking beyond particular instances to the general relations of organic life, we see how beautifully it is adapted, as it were, to lean upon the general breast of nature, and be by it continually supported and renewed. It is a channel through which the ever-present energy of nature works—an open course in which its forces may flow. All nature, indeed, to the eye that traces its hidden powers and deeper workings, is visibly pressing around the plant and compelling it to live and grow. It has simply to receive and to be passive; its labour is done for it. It toils not, neither does it spin; but it yields itself freely to obey.

CHAPTER IV.

OF LIVING FORMS; OR, MORPHOLOGY.

THE builder of an organ, it has been said, must be a wise man; and the non-mechanical part of the world will willingly concede the point. We wonder at a skill and forethought which can create from passive wood and metal an instrument so elaborately planned, so subtly tuned to harmony. It is a grand example of man's dominion over matter. So with any other mechanical triumph: we not only admire, but on man's behalf we are proud of, the chronometer, the steam-engine, the thousand contrivances for abridging labour with which our manufacturing districts abound. But suppose there were a man who could construct one or all of these under quite different conditions; who, without altering by his own exertion the operation of one of the natural laws, could bid a steam-engine arise, or a watch grow into shape ; who, while he called into existence wheel, or lever, or pipe, and fitted them into orderly connection to achieve his ends, could yet show us that the natural forces, the properties involved in the things themselves, accomplished all; and could demonstrate to us for each useful or beautiful result a chain of causation reaching to the heart of all things: were not that more wonderful—infinitely more ?

And so if we could discover for the exquisite forms of living things, for that marvellous grace of vegetable life which fills us with a wonder ever new, and a delight that familiarity cannot deaden—for the astonishing adaptations of structure in the animal frame, which, though yet but half-revealed, even science dwells on with a reverent awe—if for these things we could discover a cause that would link them with the heart of all things, should we not be glad ?   Should we not wonder, and admire, and feel that a secret not less than sacred had been revealed to us?

Life is lovely every way.   Even if we look upon it as an isolated thing, existing apart from the rest of nature, and using the inorganic world merely as a dead pedestal on which to sustain itself, it is still beautiful. Not even a narrow thought like this can strip it of its charm. But narrow thoughts like this have unhappily the power of drawing a veil around the eyes, and closing up the heart until it clings to baseless vagaries of fancy as if they were consecrated truths, and shrinks from nature's deeper teaching with superstitious dread.

How lovely life were if it were but a revealing! the bright blossom wherein nature's hidden force comes forth to display itself; the necessary outpouring of the universal life that circulates within her veins, unseen. How lovely, if life were rooted in nature's inmost being, and expressed to us in the most perfect form the meaning of the mighty laws and impulses which sway her, and which, as written on the seas, and rocks, and stars, is too vast for us to grasp: the bright and merry life, with its ten thousand voices, bursting forth from the dim and silent Law which rules the world, as in the babbling spring, the stream that has run darkling underground bursts forth and sparkles to the sun.

If we carry this thought with us, and remember
that nothing can make life less beautiful or less
divine, but that to see life essentially involved in
nature, and flowing as a necessary consequence from
her profoundest laws, would make those laws, to us,
unutterably more divine and beautiful, we can enter
into the spirit of a remonstrance which Bacon ad-
dressed to the men of his age, and may feel, perhaps,
that it is even yet not out of date :—" To say that
the hairs of the eyelids are for a quickset and fence
about the sight; or that the firmness of the skins and
hides of living creatures is to defend them from the
extremities of heat and cold; or that the bones are
for the columns, or beams, whereupon the frame of
the bodies of living creatures is built; or that the
leaves of the trees are for the protecting of the fruit;
or that the clouds are for watering of the earth; or
that the solidness of the earth is for the station and
mansion of living creatures; and the like: is well
inquired and collected in metaphysic, but in physic
they are impertinent; nay, they are indeed but
remoras and hindrances, to stay and slug the ship
from further sailing, and have brought this to pass,

that the search of the physical causes hath been neglected and passed in silence."

" The search of the physical causes has been neglected and passed in silence." Is not this still true in respect to the form and structure of living things? Partly a genuine and natural wonder at the exquisite beauty and perfection of their adaptations—which fill the mind with a sense of rest and satisfaction, as if their beauty were sufficient reason for their being, and exonerated the intellect from inquiry into the means by which they are effected—and, partly, feelings less to be commended, have stayed and slugged the ship of science from further sailing here.

But this is greatly to our loss. We cannot tell, indeed, how greatly to our loss it may be; or what insight into grand, or even materially useful laws we thus forego. This much is evident, that we lose thereby the opportunity of discovering whether there be proof of that unity of the vital and other laws, which, if it exist, it would delight and amaze us so to recognize, and which would justify us in raising to a level so much higher, our entire conception of the scheme of creation.   For it is by the discovery of the *physical* causes of the results we witness in life, that the evidence of this unity must be given.   The study of the *final* causes, or uses aimed at, true and beautiful as it is, tends rather to separate than to unite the organic and the inorganic world.   We are apt, so, to put asunder in our thought what God has joined together, and (if we are not watchful of ourselves) may seek to elevate the one by degradation of the other.

To trace the ends achieved by living forms—the adaptation of the eye to light, of the ear to sound, the dexterous grace of the hand, the stedfast balance of the foot, the strength of bone, and delicate response of nerve to Nature's lightest touch, is a delightful task, and endless as it is delightful.   To turn from this pursuit (which ever allures us on, and makes our labour its own immediate reward), and seek mere passive causes in the physical conditions which make these things necessary, might seem to be, if a needful sacrifice for science' sake, yet still a sacrifice, and a descent to lower ground.   But it is not really so. How often in our experience it happens that the apparently uninviting study becomes full of the intensest interest, and yields the richest fruit. Not the flowery meadow, but the steep and rugged path, leads to the mountain's top; and he who in studying living forms contents himself with enjoying their beauty, and tracing their design, sports like a child with flowers in the vale, and foregoes the wider horizon and the clearer day which reward him whose toilsome feet achieve the summit.

Is the study of Living Form so hard and tedious, then (and chilling too), that nothing but climbing up a mountain can be compared to it? By no means. It is of an almost incredible simplicity. And this is the wonder of it. The simplicity of the mode by which organization is brought about increases a hundredfold the wondrousness of life, and adds the new mystery of an almost inconceivable economy of means to the already overwhelming mystery of multiplicity and grandeur in the ends.

It is in life as it is in thought—the matter is furnished from one source, the form from another. Of all the expounders of a great discovery it is well known that the discoverer himself is one of the worst. Nature, in truth, divides her work, and has recourse to a twofold agency. To one man she assigns the task of originating the new thought; to another, that of imparting to it a fitting shape, and adapting it to the uses of mankind. So discoveries become known and spread. The popularizer succeeds to the philosopher, and the knowledge that would else have been wasted on a few becomes available for all. Sometimes these co-workers only succeed each other at long intervals, and secrets wrung from nature by the toil or genius of one age wait—as seeds may wait for ages ere the vivifying warmth and moisture call them into growth —for the time and the man who, at a far distant epoch, shall adapt them to the wants and understandings of the race. Sometimes, by happier chance, the expositor follows quick upon the thinker; but, quickly or slowly, he must come. The "how" is no less essential than the "what."

Just so it is in respect to life. Because it is wrought into shapes of exactest harmony, and complex and subtle adaptation, the organic world

6

bears its pre-eminence. The living matter were of
little avail without the vital form. To no purpose
were the forces of nature (grasped, as we can hardly
help thinking, in a living and friendly hand) modified into the vital mode of action, and directed to
the production of the marvellous organic substance,
if a power were not present to receive and tend it,
to mould it into beauty for delight, and knit it into
strength for use.

And what this power is, a little observation will
reveal to us. It may be traced in every wayside
plant, and lies hidden in every bud. Fig. 7, for

Fig. 7.

example, represents a leaf of the Potentilla. The
reader will observe that, while the central leaflet is
nearly symmetrical, the two lateral leaflets are very

decidedly unsymmetrical, the superior half of each
being smaller than the inferior.   It appears as if the
upper edge of the leaflet had been trimmed.   If now
we take a leaf at an earlier stage of its development,
the cause of this difference in form, or, at least, one
of its causes, will be evident.   Fig. 8 shows the bud
of a similar leaf before it has
completely unfolded.   The different leaflets are evidently not
similarly circumstanced: the lateral ones are so folded that
while their lower halves are free,
their superior halves are in contact with the central leaflet and with each other, and so are impeded in their growth.   The central leaflet, lying
equally between them, expands equally on each
side.   The common strawberry leaf shows the same
form, arising in the same way.

Fig. 8.

If we consider the leaf further, we perceive,
however, that not only are the leaflets on the sides
modified in their form by the conditions under which
they have grown, but that the central one is modified also in not less degree.   Evidently the lower

6—2

halves of the lateral leaflets exhibit the natural and
unimpeded growth of the part. The central leaflet,
though resisted equally on both sides, and therefore
symmetrical in form, yet has been formed under resistance. The free or perfect leaflet would be represented by the union of the two lower halves of the
lateral leaflets (see Fig. 9). The difference of this

Fig. 9.

Central leaflet, as in nature.   Leaf formed by the lower halves
of the lateral leaflets.

form from that of the central leaflet indicates the
effect of the pressure exerted on the latter by the
adjacent parts.

Or let us pass to another simple object. Fig. 10
represents a pea which has been made to germinate
in water. The radicle has grown freely into a
spiral form; the plumule has risen up into a curve.

Of the spiral radicle we shall speak by-and-by; at present let us look at the plumule. Would it be thought that a great and most important law in the production of organic form is here exhibited?

Fig. 10.   Fig. 11.

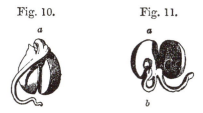

Pea which has germinated in water.—*a* Plumule. *b* Radicle.

But it is so. The reason of the bent-up form which the plumule assumes is easily discovered. The end of it is fixed by being embraced between the two halves (or cotyledons) of the pea (see Fig. 11), and the stalk, therefore, as it lengthens, necessarily grows into a projecting curve. It is a result of *growth under limit*. Does it not seem almost puerile to make matter of special observation of such a thing as this? Yes, it is puerile; it is like a child. And the kingdom of science, Lord Bacon has observed, is like the kingdom of heaven in this, that only by becoming as a child can it be entered.

Every organ of the body begins in this very way :
by a curved projection of the growing substance.

Let us look, for instance,
at the first-formed organs
in the development of the
chicken within the egg.
Figs. 12 and 13 represent

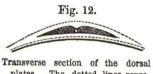

Fig. 12.

Transverse section of the dorsal
plates. The dotted lines represent the enclosing membranes
(after Wagner).

them in section : they are slight elevations, and are
called the " Dorsal Plates," because they are gradually developed into the spinal column.

These elevations are formed out of a layer of cells
called the " germinal membrane," from which all the

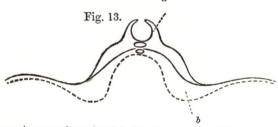

Fig. 13.

a

b

The same, at a more advanced period of development (after Todd and Bowman.)—
a Dorsal plates. b Commencement of a similar fold in another layer of
membrane.

parts of the bird are gradually evolved. It is represented in Fig. 13. Can we help asking whether this
may not be a case like that of the growing pea?
Whether these *ridges* are not formed because the

membrane is *growing under limit,* and is expanding
in length while its ends are fixed?

If we should ask this question, there are facts
which will enable us to answer it.   The layer of
cells *is* growing under limit; it is contained in a
dense capsule or external membrane, which does
interfere with its free expansion.   There is proof

Fig. 14.

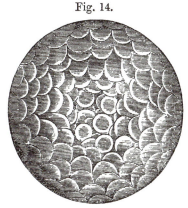

Germinal membrane, at early stage (after Bischoff); the cells rounded.

that this is the case.   Fig. 14 represents the cells of
which the germinal membrane consists when it is
first formed.   They are nearly round, and lie in
simple contact with each other.   But after a short
time, as they grow, their shape changes.   They
become pressed together by the resisting capsule,

and present a hexagonal appearance, as shown in Fig. 15. No one doubts that this change in the form

Fig. 15.

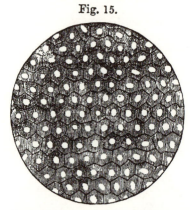

Germinal membrane, at a later period; the cells flattened by pressure.

of the cells is due to the pressure arising from their increase under limit. Can we doubt, then, that the rising up of the dorsal plates is due to the same cause? in fact, that it is just such a rising up as we see in the plumule of the pea? If we spread a handkerchief on a table, place the hands flat upon it a little way apart, and gradually bring them nearer to each other, we produce similar ridges.

The frond of a common fern again illustrates the process. Every one has noticed how it is curled,

when young (Fig. 16).   It looks as if it had been
rolled up.   But this is not the case; it may easily
be seen that it cannot be.
There has not been a flat
frond which could be curled
up.   It *grows* into this form,
because the central part
grows, while the ends are
fixed.   With the increase of
the plant it becomes free
and uncurls; but it has never
curled.   The curling is an
appearance due to its growth.

Fig. 16.

Young Frond of the Male Fern.

Or let us take another
class of forms.   The buds
of plants almost always grow in the axils of the
leaves.   It is not hard to see a reason for this.   The
axil is the interval between the leaf and the stem;
a kind of vacuity or space, into which the growing
tissues may most easily expand.   All the rest of the
surface of the stem is covered in by the hard resisting bark, but where the leaf separates this resistance
is diminished.   It is the joint in the armour.   So,

in many rapidly growing plants, if a leaf be wounded a bud springs from the spot. The wound constitutes an artificial " axil." So, again, in " budding," a wound is made to enable the new root to grow.

One reason, then, why buds come in axils surely is, that there the least resistance is offered to the expansion of the soft substance of the plant. If we turn, again, to the development of the bird, we shall find what is precisely analogous.* Very many of the organs are formed, like buds, in axils. Fig. 17 represents the young chicken at an early period of its formation ; the brain consisting then of three small lobes.

Now, in the interspaces or axils between these lobes, the eye and the ear bud out. These organs

Fig. 17.

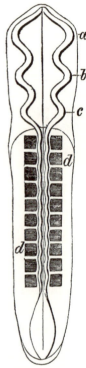

Diagram of the chicken in an early stage (after Wagner). The double lines represent the dorsal plates before described.
a anterior lobe of brain.
b middle lobe.
c posterior lobe.
d rudiments of the back-bone.

* It is the same in all vertebrate animals, but the bird is most easily examined.

grow where a free space is afforded for them, at the
points of separation between the lobes which, at this
early period, constitute the brain.   The eye " buds
out " between the first and second lobes, the ear

Fig. 18.

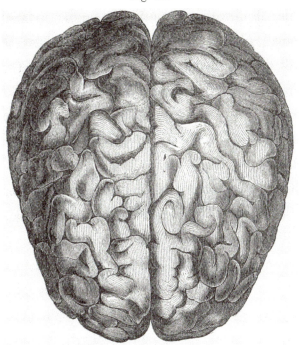

The convolutions of the brain.

between the second and third.   They are at first
hollow protrusions, merely, of the substance of the
brain.   The attached portion, or " pedicle," lengthens

and becomes relatively smaller afterwards, and constitutes respectively the optic and auditory nerve.

Or, let us look at the fully developed brain of
any of the higher mammalia. Fig. 18 is a representation of that of man. The surface is wrinkled
up in all directions, constituting quite a maze of
elevated ridges, called *convolutions*. Do not these
recall the "dorsal plates" (Fig. 12)? Are they not
evidently formed in the same way? The external
layer of the brain, expanding beneath the dense
resisting skull, is folded into these "convolutions"
for lack of space.

Surely, we have thus discovered one of the causes
of the forms of living things, in the mechanical
conditions under which they are developed. The
chemical forces, as we have seen, are used to produce the living substance; mechanical force, in the
resistance of the structures which surround the
growing organism, is used to shape it into the
necessary forms. This is nature's division of labour.
These are the simple means employed by the
Creator for bringing into being the marvels of the
organic world. Chemical force stores up the power,

the mechanical resistance moulds the structure.   We
shall see this more truly by-and-by.

For the question arises, how far this reference to
mechanical conditions may be carried.   Evidently
that cause is operative, but is it the only one?   In
answer to this question, we may say first, that, since
the mechanical conditions present during its formation do, to a certain extent, determine the structure
which the growing organism assumes, and may be
seen to produce some of the beautiful and useful
forms which it displays, we may not assume other
causes until it is proved that these are insufficient.
Here is a fact: the mechanical conditions under
which plants and animals are developed have a
power of determining their forms in the right and
necessary way.   The limit of this power must be
learnt by observation.

Or, if we look at the matter in another way, the
conclusion is equally evident.   Let us consider for
a moment the circumstances of a developing plant
or animal.   Here is the living substance; it is a
soft, plastic mass increasing in size; the forces of
nature are operating upon it, adding to its bulk.

Around it is a more or less resisting envelope.
Will it not necessarily grow in those directions in
which its extension is the least resisted? The case
is, to a certain extent, like that of taking the copy
of a medal in wax—it is a very rough comparison,
but still it may help us to grasp the general idea—
the plastic substance, under the pressure of the
artist's hand, moulds itself into the desired form by
extending where the resistance is the least. There
is no possibility of its doing otherwise. The case
is as demonstrable as a proposition in Euclid. And
it is equally so in respect to the growing plant or
animal; under the pressure arising from the increase
of its mass, it will mould itself by extending where
the resistance is the least.

But the process, of course, is much more complex
than in this simple illustration. Perpetual changes
and modifications are taking place, and especially in
this respect, that every step in the development has
its share in determining all that follow. Every
newly-formed part or organ, each minutest fold,
becomes at once a factor in the process. Thus it
is, of course, that from seeds, all of them so much

alike, their widest diversities being apparently trivial, the infinite variety of vegetable form arises. The slightest incipient diversities are continually repro- duced and multiplied, like a slight error in the beginning of a long calculation; and thus very trivial differences of form or structure between two seeds may generate an absolute unlikeness in the resulting plants.

But the true evidence of this law of living form is that which every one may find for himself. Every part of every creature, in which the means of its formation can be traced, will furnish it. If the bud of any flower be opened at an early stage, it will be seen how the petals grow into shape, modelled by the enclosing calyx; how the stamens are leaves that have not been able to unfold, and the anthers exactly fill the cavity of the bud, receiving thence their form. Or if the pod of the common pea be opened at various periods, the formation of the pea within it may be traced, under the influence of the like conditions; the plumule growing between the cotyledons when their expansion is resisted, and being itself a bud formed in an axil. Everywhere may be discerned more or less clearly a plastic expanding tissue, modelled by the varying resistances it meets.   In individual instances, no observer has been able to ignore this fact.   "I fear," says Mr. Ruskin, in a recent volume,* discussing the formation of the branches of trees by fibres descending from the leaves—"I fear the reader would have no patience with me, if I asked him to examine, in longitudinal section, the lines of the descending currents of wood, as they eddy into the increased single river.   Of course, it is just what would take place if two strong streams, filling each a cylindrical pipe, ran together into one larger cylinder, with a central rod passing up every tube.   But as this central rod increases, and at the same time the supply of the stream from above, every added leaf contributing its little current, the eddies of wood about the fork become intensely curious and interesting; of which thus much the reader may observe in a moment, by gathering a branch of any tree (laburnum shows it better, I think, than most), that

---

* *Modern Painters*, vol. v. p. 46.

the two meeting currents, first wrinkling a little, then rise in a low wave in the hollow of the fork, and flow over at the side, making their way to diffuse themselves round the stem (as in Fig. 19). Seen laterally, the bough bulges out below the fork, rather curiously and awkwardly, especially if more than two boughs meet at the same place, growing in one plane. If the reader is interested in the subject, he will find strangely complicated and wonderful arrangements of stream when smaller boughs meet larger."

Fig. 19.

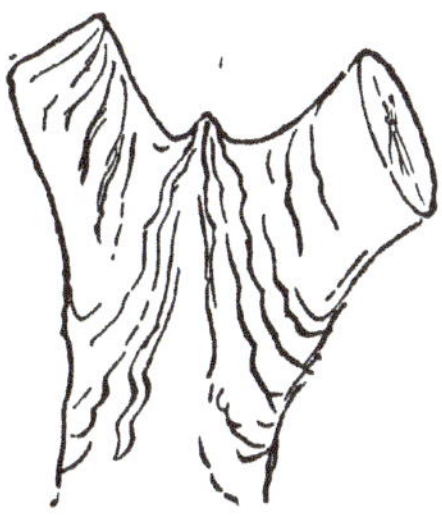

The reader will perceive how exactly this description and figure illustrate the principle. But no enumeration of instances could do justice to the evidence, or have any other effect than that of making the unlimited seem scanty. The proof is everywhere. One general fact may be referred to —the universally spiral form of organic bodies. The most superficial glance reveals a spiral tendency as a general characteristic both of the vegetable and animal creation; but a minute examination traces

7

it in every detail. An essentially spiral construction is manifested from the lowest rudiments of life, upwards throughout every organ of the highest and most complex animal. The beautifully spiral forms of the branches of many trees, and of the shells which adorn the coast, are striking examples merely of an universal law. But the spiral is the direction which a body moving under resistance ever tends to take, as may be well seen by watching a bubble rising in water, or a moderately heavy body sinking through it. They will rise or sink in manifestly spiral curves. *Growth under resistance* is the chief cause of the spiral form assumed by living things. Parts which grow freely show it well;— the horns of animals, or the roots of seeds when made to germinate in water (as shown before in Fig. 9). The expanding tissue, compressed by its own resisting external coat, wreathes itself into spiral curves. A similar result may be attained artificially by winding a thread around a leaf bud on a tree, so as to impede its expansion; it will curve itself into a spiral as it grows.

The formation of the heart is an interesting illus-

tration of the law of spiral growth.   That organ
originates in a mass of pulsating cells, which,

Fig. 20.

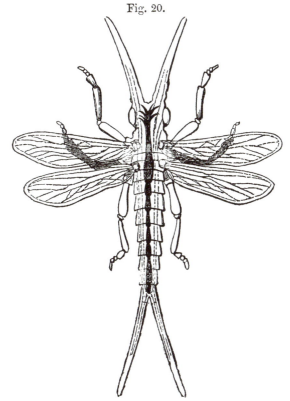

Diagram of the circulation in a winged insect. The dark central portion represents
the heart; it extends nearly the whole length of the body.

gradually becoming hollow, gives the first form of
the heart in a straight tube, more or less subdivided,
and terminating at each extremity in blood-vessels.

7—2

This is the permanent form of the heart in many animals. Fig. 20 represents the heart of an insect. When the organ is to be developed into a more complex form, the first step in the process is its twisting into the shape shown in Fig. 21. It is like what takes place when we hold a flexible rod in our hands, and gradually approximate its ends. The straight tube is growing within a limited space, and therefore " coils itself into a spiral form." And this fundamental form it retains throughout all its subsequent development.

Fig. 21.

Heart of mammal at an early stage (after Bischoff). The central expanded portion is the heart; above and below are the blood-vessels communicating with it.

But if this principle is true, why has it been overlooked? and why have men fallen into a way of speaking as if living matter had some inherent tendency to grow into certain forms, or as if masses of cells could model themselves, by some faculty or power of their own, into elaborate and complex shapes?

It seems a strange thing that they should have done so, and yet it may easily be accounted for.

The simplicity of nature's working is too profound
for man's imagination to fathom, and is revealed
only to humble seeking and steadfast self-control.
Never could men have *guessed* that through such
means such results could be achieved, even by a
skill they deemed divine. And if we ask why it
was not examined and observed long ago, the answer
is, that other causes had been invented, and men
had made up their minds. There was a " plastic
power," a " specific property," a " formative *nisus*,"
or " effort." Shall we go on with the list? Is
it any wonder that men could not see a simple,
commonplace fact like this—that living things grow
as they cannot help growing?

And, truth to say, there is all excuse for them.
Nature is a wise and patient instructress of our
ignorance. She never hurries us; but is content
that we should read her lesson at last, after we
have exhausted all our guesses. Has the reader ever
taught a child to read, or watched the process?
If so, he has seen a " great fact " in miniature; the
whole history of science on a reduced scale. For
will not the urchin do any conceivable thing rather

than look at the book? Does he not, with the
utmost assurance, call out whatever letter comes
uppermost, whatever word presents to his little
imagination the slightest semblance of plausibility?
He never looks until he cannot guess any more.

Mothers are patient, Heaven be praised; but not
so patient as our great Mother. For when the
young rogue, finding it is of no use to guess any
more, says, in mock resignation, " I can't tell," the
maternal indignation will sometimes flash forth.
But when we, finding that the mystery of life will
not yield to our hypotheses, say, " We cannot learn
it; it is a mystery insoluble," no sound of im-
patience or rebuke escapes the calm lips of Nature.
Silently as of old the great volume is spread out
before us year by year. Quietly and lovingly, as
at the first, her finger points us to the words, written
in tender herb, and stately tree, and glowing flower;
ever to our hearts repeating her simple admonition,
" Look." She knows we shall obey her when the
time is come.

But we are wandering from the subject. The
law that the mechanical conditions under which they

grow determine the form of living things, requires, like all laws, to be seen in its relations.   It does not, of course, operate alone.   The expanding germ is moulded into its shape by the resistance it meets; but the expansion has its own laws, and does not always take place equally in all directions.   For the most part, in growing organisms, the tendency to growth exists more strongly in some parts than in others; and this varying tendency depends on causes which, though they are sometimes discoverable, are not always so.   Let us revert to the case of the dorsal plates before referred to (Figs. 12 and 13). If they are caused to rise up by the expansion of the germinal membrane within its unyielding capsule, it is evident that this membrane must be growing chiefly in one direction (that at right angles to their length).   It is the same in almost every case, but this one instance will suffice.   Now this tendency to growth in particular directions is sometimes merely apparent, and arises from these being the directions in which there is least resistance to expansion.   Sometimes, however, it seems to be due to a greater intensity, in certain parts, of the forces which produce growth; as, for instance, to a local *decomposition* generating a greater energy of vital action in that part, according to the law explained in the previous chapters. In these cases, the local growth resembles the increased development of plants on the side which receives most light. And the causes of the greater energy of growth in one part than another, may be often traced back several steps; as when an increased *pressure* produces a local decomposition, and this gives rise again to a new organizing action.

Thus some apparent exceptions to the law of growth in the direction of least resistance receive an explanation. As, for example, that the root extends beneath the soil, and overcomes the resistance of the earth. The answer to this objection is, first, that the soft cellular condition of the growing radicles forbids the idea that the roots force themselves into the ground; and secondly, that their growth is accounted for by the presence in the soil of the agencies which produce growth. In truth, the formation of the root affords a beautiful illustration of the law of least resistance, for it

grows by insinuating itself, cell by cell, through
the interstices of the soil, winding and twisting
whithersoever the obstacles in its path determine,
and growing there most, where the nutritive materials
are added to it most abundantly. As we look on
the roots of a mighty tree, it appears to us as if
they had thrust themselves with giant violence into
the solid earth. But it is not so; they were led
on gently, cell added to cell, softly as the dews
descended and the loosened earth made way. Once
formed, indeed, they expand with an enormous
power, and it is probable that this expansion of the
roots already formed may crack the surrounding
soil, and help to make the interstices into which
the new rootlets grow. Nor is there any good
reason for assuming that the roots encounter from
the soil a greater resistance to their growth than
the portions of the stem meet with from other causes.
We must not forget the hard external covering
of the parts exposed to air and light. In some
classes of palms this resistance is so great that the
growth of the tree is stopped by it.

Similar to the case of the root are those in which

mushrooms have been known to lift up heavy masses
by their growth, sometimes raising in a single night
a stone weighing many pounds. The forces which
produce growth operate with enormous power. And
well they may; for they are essentially the same
forces—those arising from the chemical properties
of bodies—which in our own hands produce the
most powerful effects, and are often indeed so violent
in their action as to be wholly beyond our control.
But it is clear that such cases as this can offer no
difficulty in respect to the laws of growth. Every
one must see that the mushroom would certainly
not have raised the stone if that had not been the
direction in which its expansion was resisted least.
In this respect, the case seems precisely similar to
the expansion of steam in a boiler raising the piston.
The mechanical resistance yields when the invisible
inward force reaches a proportionate amount.

There is, however, another class of instances to
which we must refer. These are the forms which
result not directly from growth but from decay, and
of which the spongy pith of many plants is an
example. The irregular cells and plates of which

the pith consists are due to the drying up and shrink-
ing of the pulp. In many animal structures this
wasting process is accompanied by a contraction of
the surrounding parts, and results in forms which
can easily be traced to their causes.

CHAPTER V.

LIVING FORMS.—THE LAW OF FORM.

THESE few instances, which might be indefinitely multiplied, may suffice to make it manifest that organic forms are to be ascribed to causes essentially the same as those which regulate the forms of inorganic bodies: in short, to the laws which force obeys wherever it is found. The peculiar structure which living bodies assume is due to the mechanical conditions under which they are placed, and not to a peculiar power operating to that special end. That peculiar power is, indeed, disproved, if further disproof were needed, by the existence of monstrosities and deformities, in which the end is not attained. The case is like that of the old doctrine that nature abhorred a vacuum.

It was found that this was true only to a certain extent, and to varying degrees; just so does the special formative power supposed in living bodies produce peculiar forms only to a limited and varying degree of accuracy.

A word may be said here, also, respecting the doctrine of " types," or standards, to which all living forms are referred. As a guide to the investigation of the organic world, this idea has proved itself invaluable; and the doctrine of corresponding parts in different organisms, to which it has been made subservient, constitutes, and must continue to constitute, a beautiful branch of physiological science.* But it is hardly necessary to say that no formative power is to be ascribed to those types or standards. The body needs some efficient cause to determine its form just as much, being conformed to such a type, as it would if it were not so conformed. Constancy of form proves constancy of conditions, and must do so equally upon every hypothesis.

---

* These corresponding parts are called " homologous ; " as, for example, in plants, leaves and stamens are homologous ; they correspond in their nature, although performing different offices.

But, in truth, neither general arguments, nor
even an array of instances, are needed to give
conclusiveness to the evidence that the forms of
living bodies are mechanically determined. Startling
as the proposition may seem when it is first uttered,*
we no sooner clearly grasp the conception and see
what it means, than it becomes self-evident.   It
is, indeed, an axiom, and is capable of being expressed in the most simple terms.   The phenomena
of organization are in this respect an instance of
the necessary characters of motion.   For it is the
nature of motion that it takes the direction of least
resistance.   This is less a " law " of motion than
a part of its definition.   No law can be imposed
on it, which can override this character ; for that
would be to alter the nature of motion itself : it
would be to assert for it a self-directive power.
In truth, the law of least resistance is involved in

---

* The surprise with which it affects us is similar to that which
we feel, or might well feel, when we reflect that our sensations of
light or colour, of music or of warmth, are referred to motion.
The cause appears altogether inadequate to the effect.   But we
have in science to accept many such strange things as at least
scientifically true.

the very meaning of the words, for by " resistance " is meant that which, preventing, thereby directs the motion.   So that, in fact, we may look at the question of organic form from another point of view, and obtain an assurance respecting the mode of its production which might be independent of experimental evidence.

For it is clear that organic forms are the result of motion.   By this expression, indeed, nothing more is meant than that, as we consider form to depend upon the position of the particles of which any body consists, so, in the case of organic bodies, these particles must have assumed their various positions by moving into them.   And since it is the inevitable nature of motion to take the direction of least resistance, it is equally clear that organic forms are the result of motion in the direction of least resistance.   Which proposition, again, is only putting into a general formula the result to which observation has led us.   In fact, here, as so often elsewhere, we first discover a truth in nature and then see that it is necessary.

Organic forms, like all natural forms whatever,

must be the result of motion in the direction of least resistance. I am aware, however, that this may seem to be, though a true, yet a one-sided statement. For though motion cannot but take the direction of least resistance, yet it is determined, not only by the resistances it meets, but even more directly and decisively by the original impulse which occasions it. Every motion has, at any given moment, an existing course, or arises from a force operating in a given direction; and the impulse of this force may be sufficient to carry it through, and cause it to overcome, great resistance, even though in other directions there may be less or none. The very use of a bullet or cannon-ball, for example, is to overcome resistance. But the deficiency in the form of the axiom when thus regarded is but apparent, and arises from our confining our view within too narrow a sphere: when we take all the conditions into consideration, it appears to be sufficiently ample and exact.

It is true there is a certain direction possessed by every existing motion, or given to every motion at its origin; but we must remember that we may not arbitrarily fix our attention on any one point, and take that as a commencement. There is no origin, or first, in nature: it is to the intellect a chain without beginning as without end. Every point of time is in this respect like every other; nor when we tax our imagination to the utmost, can we approximate in the least degree nearer to the beginning than we are now. That divine act, to which all events are to be ascribed as their true cause, may be associated as well—quite as rationally and assuredly much more devoutly—with that part of the sequence which is present now, as with any we can conceive to have been in the past.

Whatever direction, therefore, any motion may possess at any time, it has been assumed under the same conditions as guide its subsequent course. The law that motion takes the direction of least resistance has prevailed from the first, and has given to it that direction in which we see it operate. The same may be said in respect to those impulses or forces from which particular motions arise: these also have been determined by that very necessity of motion which they may appear to supersede. We see an instance

8

of this in the bullet or cannon ball, supposed before. The gun is an instrument for giving, by a definite resistance, a certain direction to motion. And so in every case; it only needs that we should not arbitrarily limit our thought, but should consent to carry our eye indefinitely back. Whatever we may suppose concerning the primary origination of motion, of every motion which we can perceive, or conceive, we must say that it is such as it is because motion takes the direction of least resistance.

And if every motion comes thus within the sphere of this law, so also, when it is rightly regarded, does the other fact referred to as apparently opposed to it —that of resistance being overcome by impulse. In this, too, there is only an apparent exception to the law of least resistance, and it arises likewise from an arbitrary limitation of our view. Giving the proposition its due extension, these cases are instances of the law, and not exceptions to it. For what is it that resists motion but force? and what is force but that which, if unresisted, produces motion? It is, therefore, motion or the cause of it that is the true resistance to motion: as when the two hands are pressed together, each mutually resists the other. Thus we of course include the impulse of the moving body among the resistances to be considered, and the axiom assumes the utmost logical completeness. An opposing resistance deflects or changes motion, or is overcome by it, according as it is greater or less than the resistance to such change presented by the motion itself. For the force of that motion clearly becomes a resistance in relation to such change or deflection.

So much it has been necessary to say with respect to the general proposition, to make clear its bearing in respect to those obvious motions with which we can best deal in thought. The argument is precisely the same in respect to those minute motions of particles in which the growth of living bodies consists. These also are determined by the same necessity, and take place equally in the direction of least resistance. Organic form, therefore, is the result of motion in the direction of least resistance : the proposition is absolute, and though first revealed by observation, is independent of it.

This general form of the proposition has the ad-

vantage of applying not only to the formation of
living bodies, in so far as it is affected by conditions arising within themselves, or by resistances immediately operative on them in their expansion; it is
capable of including, when viewed in its wider
aspects, all the external forces which are concerned
in determining their forms. For all those forces
have themselves arisen under the law of least resistance. In order to bring them within the same
formula, we need only extend our thought and take
into our regard a wider sphere. The resistances we
have to consider are not only those which are immediately related to the growing organism, but those
which exist throughout all nature. When we view the
living thing in its cosmical, its world-wide relations,
we may state in absolutely unlimited terms, that its
form is determined by motion in the direction of the
least resistance. That law has made it necessary,
has carried it in its bosom from the first, and in due
time has brought it forth.

Mr. Herbert Spencer, in his *First Principles*, has
done me the honour to refer to my arguments on this
subject (as stated in the British and Foreign Medico-

Chirurgical Review, for October, 1858), in terms of approbation. He urges, however, that the line of organic growth is rather the result of tractive and resistant forces combined than determined by resistance alone. I may remark on this, that I did not design to ignore the operation of the former class of agencies. In the paper alluded to, I say: "The growth or expansion must exist before any question can arise of the direction it shall take; the molecular actions which result in organic increase must be presupposed. Now, these molecular actions come into operation under laws which are doubtless fixed and determinate, and which it may not be impossible to ascertain, but of which no account is attempted here. In the germinating seed, the vital action commences first, and exists most powerfully, in the radicle; the root, therefore, has the first tendency to grow. From this point the application of the law of living form commences. It is the more necessary to bear in mind this consideration, because it is of universal application. In almost all cases of growth or development, the vital action manifests itself in some parts rather than in others; it exhibits foci, as it were, of greatest energy. It is only by duly marking these, that the effect of mechanical conditions in determining form can be appreciated." And again: " If it should be remarked that there exist in developing structures certain definite modes or operations of force, such as attractions or repulsions in particular directions, which serve to determine the form assumed, apart from any influence of visible mechanical conditions, this is willingly admitted to be true. The law suggested does not contravene, but rests upon these phenomena. They may be regarded in two ways: either as instances of those local manifestations of growth before referred to, and which are presupposed as the foundation on which the law is based; or, perhaps, more properly, they may be themselves considered as coming within its scope. In so far as these changes consist in the motion of particles, the law of least resistance may be asserted of them, or at least cannot be denied. Such molecular changes indeed form no part of the evidence on which the proposition can be based; inasmuch as the nature of the process and all its conditions are as yet beyond our investigation. But that in so far

as they consist in motion, they conform to the nature
of motion we may be quite sure. The *structure* of the
germ must be such as to determine the operation of
whatever chemical or other forces come into play within
it, to produce motion in these particular directions."

I have thus sought to leave the door open to any
other agencies, the operation of which in determining
form it might be found necessary to recognize. But
from the foregoing remarks, it will be seen that I
believe there is another mode of regarding the subject, in which all these agencies may be viewed as
instances of the law of least resistance, and by an
extension of the sphere of vision become included
among the very phenomena to which they appear as
an exception. Under the one aspect the living
structure is regarded by itself; in which case two,
or more, laws are concerned in determining its form;
under the other, it is viewed as a part, and in relation to the whole of external nature, and then all the
forces affecting its structure come within one formula. It would be an error to look on these two
modes of regarding the subject as opposed. Each is
appropriate to its own object.

Several instances of the result of external forces in modifying the forms of plants and animals have been collected by Mr. Spencer.* The following is one of his examples :—

"If we examine a common fir-tree—and I choose a fir-tree, because the regularity in its mode of growth makes the law more than usually manifest—we shall find that the uppermost branches, which grew out of the leading shoot, have radially arranged branchlets (*i. e.* growing equally on all sides), and each of them repeats on a smaller scale the type of the tree itself. But if we examine branches lower and lower down the tree, we find the vertically growing branchlets bear a less and less ratio to the horizontally growing ones. Shaded and confined by those above them, these eldest branches develop their offshoots in those directions where there are most space and light; becoming finally quite flattened and fan-shaped. The like general truth is readily traceable in other trees."

In this connection, it is impossible to omit a reference also to the beautiful experiments by which

* In the *British and Foreign Medico-Chirurgical Review* for January, 1859.

Mr. Rainey has demonstrated the operation of physical laws in the production of shell and bone. By causing the gradual formation of carbonate of lime in a viscid fluid, such as a solution of gum, that physiologist has succeeded in obtaining globules consisting partly of organic and partly of mineral matter, which correspond indistinguishably with the forms presented in the development of the shells or skeletons of certain animals.

It is remarkable, also, to how great an extent the power of spontaneous repair of injuries resolves itself into an exhibition of the law of growth in the direction of least resistance. Is not a wound virtually an "axil?" and the granulations which form in it, or the new member which grows in the place of a lost one, do not they correspond to the buds which form in axils in the growth of plants, or the development of the embryo? The wound removes the resistance of the external investiture of the body. No special power, therefore, appears to be needed, by which a living body should be enabled to recover itself from accident or injury. The law of its formation involves also its repair. So, if the leaves of some plants be incised, buds spring up from the cut surface; or a new hydra grows from a wound in its parent: an artificial axil being made. Other circumstances, doubtless, are concerned in repair; but the general fact is a simple exhibition of the mechanical direction of growth. The new material is accumulated where the resistance to expansion is removed: —is it not deposited there rather than in other portions of the body, because the resistance at that point is the least? We know that repair is effected at the expense of the general nutrition of the body: and we know, too, the effect of pressure in limiting it. At least we may say this: that if this law of growth be true, then it is certain (other circumstances being the same) that wounds must be repaired.

Dr. Macvicar has adduced very striking arguments to show that the natural forces, regarded in their most general aspect, tend to the production of the sphere —the most perfect form—and that the phenomena of organic development are, to a very large extent, interpretable from this point of view. "It is precisely those forms which geometry shows to be most highly endowed, that natural bodies tend to emulate in their forms, as they themselves become more perfect, the physical forces in their various modes of operation constituting a machinery framed expressly to realize these forms."* He refers to the counteracting yet co-operating effects of gravity and of heat, drawing or expanding matter alike into spherical forms; and points out how living bodies, almost without exception, consist of cells which are spherical, except where changed by pressure; and how all organic forms exhibit a spherical tendency more or less modified by interfering causes. But we could not do justice to his arguments without quoting all his words; and, indeed, without going farther, may we not sum up the lesson of these various investigations in the words of the great American physiologist, Dr. J. W. Draper:—" The problems of organization are not to be solved by empirical schemes; they require the patient application of all the aids that can be furnished by all other branches of human knowledge, and even then the solution comes tardily. Yet there is no cause for us to adopt those quick but vision-

---

* *The Economy of Nature; or, First Lines of Science simplified.* Appendix, p. 108.

ary speculations, or to despair of giving the true explanation of all physiological facts. Since it is given us to know our own existence, and be conscious of our own individuality, we may rest assured that we have, what is in reality a far less wonderful power, the capacity of comprehending all the conditions of our life. Then, and not till then, will man be a perfect monument of the wisdom and power of his Maker, a created being knowing his own existence, and capable of explaining it."

CHAPTER VI.

IS LIFE UNIVERSAL?

" MAN capable of explaining his own existence!" I seem to hear the reader exclaim, as he peruses the eloquent passage borrowed from Dr. Draper, in our last chapter; " it is a vain dream; we shall never be able to say what life is." Perhaps not; yet we should not be too hasty in deciding on this negative. Nothing can seem more improbable, as that question has been put, than that it should ever receive a satisfactory reply; but may there not have been an error in the way of putting it? Problems that are truly simple sometimes come before us in a very difficult form, owing to pre-conceptions in our minds, and demand for their solution not great ingenuity or power, but that we should disembarrass ourselves of false persuasions. One of the greatest intellects has left on record the maxim—it is part of the rich legacy bequeathed by the author of the *Novum Organon*—that " a wise seeking is the half of knowing." According to our first impression, a wide gulf separates that which has life from that which has not. We naturally, therefore, prejudge the very point at issue, and assume in living things the possession of a peculiar endowment, which is the cause of all that is distinctive in them. And then, with this idea in our minds, we strive in vain to untie the knot. The more we seek to understand life, considered as a power capable in itself of effecting the various results which are exhibited in organic bodies —their growth, development and repair, their form and structure, their continued existence in spite of opposing agencies, their power of assimilating extraneous substances and making them part of themselves—the more convinced we become that it can never be understood.

And the difficulty is immensely increased by the connection which exists between life and *consciousness*. The union of mind and body is in our experience so intimate and so incessant, that we naturally think of them together. Hence it arises that quite foreign considerations, affecting the spiritual nature of man, ever tend to exert a disturbing influence on the higher questions of physiology. It is not easy to keep separate in our thoughts the purely physical life of the body, and the spiritual faculties of feeling and will to which it is subservient.

But distinguishing the mental and the material life, and fixing our thoughts upon the body, over which, as over an obedient instrument, the conscious man bears sway, we may see the path to be pursued. Life exhibits, not the agency of a single power, but the united effects of several causes: the problem of vitality requires division into various simpler problems. We have to seek not the nature of an invisible agent, but the demonstrable causes of a vast variety of physical results. We have found, for example, three prominent questions claim an answer in respect to the living body: how it acts; why it grows; and whence its form? Taking these questions one by one, and seeking guidance from the facts presented to us by nature, we have also found that each of them was capable of a solution simple enough, and even obvious when once it was seen. We may briefly recapitulate the results at which we have arrived.

I. Living bodies GROW by the operation of chemical force, which exhibits in them a twofold action, and produces substances which tend to decompose; on the same principle that gravitation in a fountain causes water to rise by the effect of its fall. So chemical change, or decomposition, causes the nourishment of the body, and the two opposite processes of growth and decay proceed in mutual dependence. This law is easily understood by fixing the thoughts on any case in which an action of one kind produces another that is opposite to itself: the movement of a pendulum, for example, in which the downward motion produces the upward, and the upward furnishes the conditions under which the downward can again take place. It is thus chemical action produces the vital action; and the vital action furnishes the conditions under which the chemical action can again take place. Living bodies, then, grow through decay, or through chemical processes which are equivalent to decay, and which resemble it in producing force.

II. The body, thus growing, receives its FORM or structure from the conditions under which it is placed in its development. Under the influence of the forces which are operating upon it, and which excite its growth, the germ expands (for the most part in certain directions more powerfully than in others); and by the varying resistances it meets in this expansion, is moulded into its specific form.

III. This form adapts it to its FUNCTIONS. The body tends to decompose, or to undergo chemical changes which give rise to force. The absorption of power in nutrition, and the evolution of it again in the decomposition of the tissues (the muscles, brain, &c.), "is precisely analogous to that which takes place in forcibly separating the poles of two magnets, retaining them apart for a certain time, and suffering them to return by their attractive force to their former union. The energy developed in the approach of the magnets towards each other is exactly equal to the force expended in their separation." In the case of the living body, the force thus developed

within it necessarily produces the actions to which its
structure is adapted.

Thus, for example, when a seed is placed in the
ground, the first process which takes place within it
is one of decomposition.   The mass of the seed consists of starch and albumen, in the midst of which is
placed a small cellular body, called the germ.   This
germ will grow, and develop into the future plant,
but only on condition that a process of decay goes on
in the starchy and albuminous matter with which it
is in connection.   Part of the latter sinks into the
inorganic state, uniting with oxygen, and passing off
as carbonic acid.   The young plant is at first of less
weight than the seed or root which has disappeared
in generating it.

When it arrives at the surface of the soil, a new
process commences.   The rays of the sun, falling on
its leaves, maintain in them a continuance of the
same process (one of chemical change) by which the
first development of the germ was determined.   Thus
new materials are added to the plant, the light exciting those chemical processes which produce the
organic arrangement of fresh portions of matter.

The leaves, under the stimulus of the sun's rays, decompose carbonic acid, giving off part of the oxygen, and " fix," as it is said, the carbon in union with hydrogen, and sometimes with nitrogen, &c., to form the various vegetable cells and their contents. It is curious that the oxygen and hydrogen, thus united with the carbon, are very often in the same proportion in which they unite to form water. Starch and sugar, for example, both consist of carbon and (the elements of) water.

An animal now consumes this plant. In digestion there takes place again a precisely similar process to that with which we started—the germination of the seed. The substance of the plant partially decomposes ; a portion of it sinks into a state approximating to the inorganic, while another portion (doubtless, by means of the force thus generated) becomes more highly vitalized, and fitted to form part of the animal structure. The germination of the seed, and animal digestion, are parallel processes. Each of them is twofold—a decomposing and a vitalizing action going on together, the latter having its origin in and depending upon the former.

9—2

Having formed part of the animal structure for a time, this living matter decomposes yet again, and again gives off its force. But now, instead of effecting, as in the previous cases, a vitalizing action, the force produces a mechanical action in the muscles, or a nervous action in the brain, or, in short, the *function* of whatever organ the matter we are tracing may have been incorporated with;—the function being but another mode of operation of the same force which caused the nutrition.

And thus, supposing the action to have been a muscular exertion, say the lifting of a weight, we shall have traced the force, which came from the inorganic world at first, in the form of the sun's rays, and was embodied in the substance of the plant, back again into the inorganic world in the form of motion.

Let us observe another thing. In previous chapters the function and the nutrition of the body have been distinguished from each other, and even contrasted.*

* To guard against misapprehension, it is as well to say that by the term *nutrition* are not intended any of the actions connected with the taking of food, but only those minute internal changes by which the growth and repair of the body are effected.

They are opposites :—the one is the formation of the body, the other depends on its destruction. And for either to be understood, it is necessary that the distinction between them should be clearly apprehended. But when we take a larger view, the relation of these two processes assumes quite a different aspect. The appearance of opposition is merged in a wider unity. The nutrition and the function of a living body are rather a twofold presentation of one process, than two different processes. That which, seen on one side, is nutrition, seen on the other is function. Let us take, first, the case in which a decomposition within the body, itself produces an increased nutrition. Here, it is evident, the increased vitality is the equivalent of a force that, if directed through the muscles, might have been productive of motion. It is, in fact, an internal function, so to speak. The force set free by decomposition in the body, instead of operating externally, operates within it. Nutrition, though it is the basis and provision for the external functional activity, may itself be classed as a function, and may take rank in the same list with the other results of internal decomposition—motion, animal heat, &c.

The case is the same as when, in a chronometer, part of the force of the unbending spring is employed to bend a secondary one.

But in another respect, also, nutrition may be seen to be identical with function. The very same process which is the function of one body, is the nutrition of another. The vegetable world, in so far as it serves for food, has for its "function," in the strictest sense, the nutrition of the animal. This is the result which it effects by its regulated decomposition. The animal instinct provides the conditions under which the function of the vegetable is performed. The plant yields up its life to nourish the animal body, as that body, so nourished, in its activity yields up *its* life to impart force to the world around.

And this is but an illustration of a law which has its basis in the very nature of force itself. Every giving off of force has for its necessary effect the storing up of force in equal amount elsewhere. The two halves of this process cannot be divided. And whichever half of it we may be at any time regarding—whether the storing up of force (which answers to nutrition), or the giving it off (which answers to function)—we may be sure that the other is also present. That which is to one thing the storing up of force, must be the giving off of force to another. We shall perceive it as either, according to the view we are taking at the time. The storing up of force within the animal frame usurps to itself, especially, the name of nutrition, because our regard naturally centres upon ourselves and upon that which is most kindred to us.

But it might be that beings, different from ourselves, should look upon the other side of this process, and see in the animal nutrition rather a loss than a gain of force—a dying rather than a coming into life. Nature in this respect is like the books of a commercial firm. When there is no change in the total, however the various amounts may be shifted, there is necessarily always an equal loss and gain, and each change will be regarded as one or the other according to the interests affected. Surely it is but fair that we should recognize this rigid equity, and try to look upon ourselves, sometimes, as if through alien eyes. We are but borrowers from Nature's store, and what she showers on us with open hand with a stern clutch she snatches from our fellows. But we are honest debtors, and pay to the last farthing.

Besides the three points to which we have directed our attention, there are very many other questions which living bodies suggest, and which equally deserve inquiry—the causes, for example, of the difference between the animal and the vegetable, or between the various textures of which our own bodies consist; by what physical necessity bone is formed in one part, muscle in another, and nerve in a third: why the circulating fluid of plants, as a rule, contains *green* particles, and that of animals *red* ones, these being complementary colours, which together constitute white light: how the various changes which take place in the gradual development of the organism, from childhood to adult life, are effected, and to what deep principle of universal order they conform. These and innumerable other subjects, which physiology presents on every hand, claim, and doubtless would well repay our pains.

But looking only to the conclusions indicated above, do they not advance us a step towards a

better understanding of the living body ? Do they
not, at least, enable us to perceive that the main
phenomena which it presents, are examples of the
same laws and properties with which our experience
of other things makes us familiar ? In other words,
do not we see that organic life is not a new thing,
as compared with that which is met with in the
inorganic world, but a new form of the same things ?
The same forces operate, the same laws rule, in the
case of organic and inorganic structures ; the results
are so different because the conditions differ. It has
been suggested before that the animal body, in
respect to its power of acting, presents an analogy to
a machine ; and the idea seems capable of receiving
a still wider application. What is a machine but a
peculiar method of applying common forces and
universal laws? We perceive this at once if we
consider any particular case. In making and using
a machine, we add nothing and we alter nothing,
in respect to the nature and properties of things.
We do but use for a particular end the powers which
exist around us, and the laws which are universally
operative. Nay, so far is a machine from involving

new forces, or new laws, it is precisely by virtue of the unaltering laws and force of nature, that it can be constructed and kept in operation. As a machine, it is dependent upon, and an example of, the laws which prevail without it; if they ceased or changed their operation, its adaptation and its power were lost. The case is the same with the living body. This also is dependent on, and is an example of, the laws and forces which prevail without it. If the laws of inorganic nature changed or ceased, if the forces of inorganic nature were no longer what they are, the animal structure would be of use, it would even exist, no more. The organic world does not differ from the inorganic in its essence.

But it differs. It would be a fatal error—happily it is an impossible one—to confound the two. There is a difference in the mode of operation, though the elements are the same. The physical powers have received in the organic world a particular direction, and are made to work to certain re- sults which are attainable only through living structures.

Surely here, then, we are in possession, up to a

certain point, of a clear and definite answer to the
question, What is Life? Ever remembering that we
speak of the bodily life only, may we not reply: It
is a particular mode of operation of the natural forces
and laws? We can trace the force operative in life,
to and fro, between organic and inorganic bodies;
we can see that in the organic world the laws we
know in the inorganic are still supreme. But the
results are new.

Thus, it is easy to understand how there has arisen
the conception of a peculiar vital Entity, or Principle.
This was a rapid generalization before the working
of the various forces that conspire in life had been
discerned. For the peculiar results, a peculiar agent
was supposed, instead of a peculiar mode of operation. Not that this conception has been universal.
Individual men have urged reasons in favour of
a different view, at various times. One of the most
notable instances is that of Coleridge, who, in his *Essay
towards the Formation of a more Comprehensive Theory
of Life* (though giving utterance to some opinions
which are doubtful or obscure), seems to have antici-
pated, so far as his general view is concerned, almost

the entire advance of physiological knowledge since his day.

His idea (derived, it is said, originally from Schelling) is, that physical life is a process, or a mode of operation, of the same powers which we recognize under other names, as magnetism, electricity, or chemical affinity. These, by their own properties, effect all the results observed in life, but they are grouped in a special way, the various forms of action being so united as to constitute, out of many parts, a mutually dependent whole. The distinctive character of living things is the exhibition in them of a "principle of individuation," which constitutes them units, separated from, while yet partakers in, that which is around them. "Life," he says, "supposes an universal principle in nature with a limiting power in every particular animal, constantly acting to individualize, and, as it were, figure the former. Thus, life is not a thing, but an act and process." And tracing the chain of organic being upward through its various grades, he points out how the great characteristic of advancing elevation in the scale of life, consists in the ever more perfect individualization of the creature; its being marked off from the rest of nature, and placed in an attitude of freedom to use and subordinate her powers.

But this subordination is not effected by the superaddition of a new power in living things. The subjection of the physical to the vital forces resembles rather a voluntary self-control than a coercion from without. The power on each side is the same. Does not the following passage from Coleridge, indeed, convey an argument that finally disposes of the idea that the force of organic bodies can be essentially different from that of the surrounding world; that being the very force which they live by assimilating or drawing into themselves?—

"To a reflecting mind the very fact, that the powers peculiar to life in living animals, include coherence, elasticity, &c. (or, in the words of a recent publication ' that living matter exhibits these physical properties ') would demonstrate, that in the truth of things they are of the same kind, and that both classes are but degrees, and different dignities of one and the same tendency. For the latter are

not subjected to the former as a lever or walking-stick
to the muscles: the more intense the life is, the less
does elasticity, for instance, appear as elasticity: it
sinks down into the nearest approach to its physical
form by a series of degrees, from the contraction and
elongation of the irritable muscle, to the physical
hardness of the insensitive nail. The lower powers
are assimilated, not merely employed, and assimilation supposes the like nature of the thing assimilated;
else it is a miracle; only not the same as that of
creation, because it would imply that additional and
equal miracle of annihilation. In short, all the im-
possibilities which the acutest of the Reformed
divines have detected in the hypothesis of transub-
stantiation would apply in the very same words to
that of assimilation, if the objects and the agents
were really of unlike kinds. Unless, therefore,
a thing can exhibit properties which do not belong to
it, the very admission that living matter exhibits
physical properties includes the further admission,
that those physical or dead properties are themselves
vital in essence, really distinct, but in appearance only
different, or in absolute contrast with each other."

The term "Principle of Individuation" admirably expresses the distinguishing characteristic of the animal body. Its force is, as it were, contained or reflected within itself. Gathered from nature in nutrition, the force which the organic matter embodies, instead of passing freely onwards, is retained and stored up within it. And the structure into which the growing organism is moulded, causes that force, when it is set free, to effect actions which subserve the well-being of the animal. And not only so, but this very force, when it is given off, by decomposition, within the body, may be reflected back upon the organism itself, and cause its increased growth; the decay, as we have seen, renewing the nutrition. Is there any way of expressing these facts more appropriate than to say that in the animal body the force is turned upon itself—self-centered? It is "individualized;" limited within definitely marked bounds. Nothing is there which is not elsewhere in nature, but a limit is applied to that which elsewhere is freely circulating.

Again it is like a machine. We cannot help perceiving the analogy; for in a machine the very

same thing is done. The forces which are freely
circulating through material things are seized by
man, and *limited*. They are bound up, and retained,
to be used for certain purposes alone. A " principle
of individuation " is brought into play ; and an instrument, or " organ " is the result. " Individuate "
the forces of nature, and we have an instrument.
The chief of instruments, the living body, presented
ready to each one of us to preserve and use, is
constituted thus.

It adds greatly to the interest with which the animal
creation may be contemplated, to look upon it with
this thought in our minds. To feel the subtle links
that tie together the diverse forms of Nature's
energy, and recognize, in the sportive youth or
vigorous maturity of bird and beast, tokens of the
same powers that make firm the earth beneath their
tread, give fluency to the waves, and cunningest chemistry to the all-embracing, all-purifying air, opens
to the lover of the animated tribes a new delight.
Not aliens are they to the earth on which they dwell,
not strangers seeking temporary lodgment and con-
venience, but in truest sense earth's children, with

the child's claim to shelter in the bosom which sustains them all.   Bone of her bone, flesh of her flesh, breath of her breath.   Each thrilling wave of life flows warm and fresh, from fountains which the sunbeams feed, which roll through every fibre of the solid globe, and spring up glowing from the central fires.

We do not require, for organic life, to assume any new or special power ; the common and all-pervading powers of nature are enough.   But now a question arises : How can the living be derived from that which is not living?   How can any limiting, or directing, or adapting, make life to be where life was not ?   This is a legitimate question.   Men refuse to rest satified with any supposition which seems to refer life to an unliving source, or to reduce it to the play of mere mechanic forces.   Often have the instincts of our nature repudiated the resolution of vital phenomena into the shifting balance of attractions, the lifeless affinities whose sweep is bounded by the chemist's crucible.   And the feeling has a just foundation; organic life cannot spring merely from dead matter.   But if the demand for a living source of life is just, it is to be observed that

10

this demand can be satisfied in two ways:—Either the material world is dead and life does not spring from it; or, *if life springs from it, then it is not dead.* If it be proved that the forces and laws of the inorganic world constitute all that is to be found of physical power or principle in organic life, then does not the conclusion follow that the apparently inorganic world is truly living too?

This is no paradox. It is not even a novelty. That Nature is universally living is a position that has often been maintained; but evidence of its truth could not be given until various physiological problems had been at least approximately solved. Let us first conceive the case hypothetically. That which constitutes matter living, in the ordinary sense, is a certain arrangement of its elements, in relations opposed, more or less, to their chemical tendencies. This arrangement of the elements gives rise to a substance in which there exists a tendency to decompose—the organic substance. This substance, moulded into adapted structures, constitutes an organic body. The conditions essential to organic life are, then, these two: an opposition to chemical affinity in the arrangement of the elements, and a structure adapted to the performance of the necessary functions. Now we must, in the present state of our knowledge, consider the living body, like all other material substances, to consist of " atoms"—minute particles, beyond which we cannot conceive division to be carried. These atoms, by their arrangement, constitute the organic matter; and if we reflect, we see that they themselves, separately considered, are not organic. They are simply the materials out of which the living body is built up, and are the same in the most highly organized animal as in the simplest mineral. The ultimate atoms of oxygen and hydrogen, for example, are the same in the human brain as they are in water; the living substance is necessarily made up of particles which are not themselves living. In other words: Physical life is a living relation of unliving parts. The ultimate atoms of which a living body is composed are not individually possessors of life; the life is in their mutual connection.

This form of life, which depends upon an opposition to chemical affinity, and therefore rests upon

that affinity as its basis and condition, is peculiar to
animal and vegetable bodies, and may be called, for
the sake of distinction, "organic life." In this kind
of life it is evident that any forms of matter which
are constituted according to the laws of chemical
affinity, do not partake. Such are the mass of our
own globe, and in all probability the other bodies
known to us as the stars and planets. These are
not partakers of the life which we have called
organic.

But if we think of nature on a larger scale, we
remember that there is another property, or tendency
of matter, cognate to chemical affinity, but affecting
masses as well as atoms. Why should not *gravity*
afford the conditions requisite for an organic relation
of the masses of which the universe consists? We
know there also exists a force opposed to gravity,
which produces an arrangement of the heavenly
bodies in relations different from that in which
gravity tends to place them. Why should not this
force constitute, in respect to them, a true analogue
of the vital force? It has been suggested that the
distances of the stars from each other are probably

not greater, in proportion, than those which separate the particles of what we call solid matter, and that the stellar universe might present, to senses of proportionate scope, an appearance like that which solids present to us. A group of stars may thus be regarded as constituting a substance—why not a vital substance ? We certainly know it to be full of the intensest activities, and to be the seat, especially, of two counteracting forces. Why should not this " substance" be moulded, also, into truly vital forms? In short, why should not the multitude of stars constitute one or more living wholes ? Would they not thus present to us a strict parallel to the " living wholes" which we have long recognized to be such —unliving particles in living relations to each other? True, the earth we live on is inorganic : true, we have good reason to conclude all the orbs contained in space to be inorganic too. This is no reason that they are not " particles"—atoms—though inorganic by themselves, in an organization of a corresponding magnitude. The atoms of which our own bodies consist, also, are " inorganic by themselves."

" An organization," I said, " of corresponding

magnitude." I am not the first to use the term.
The "organization" of the heavens—of our own
solar system, and of the various galaxies of stars—
has been often spoken of. The likeness of the stellar
groups, and of their ordered and recurrent move-
ments, to the forms and processes of the organic
world, has found for itself a voice, at least in meta-
phor. There is a striking passage in the first volume
of *Cosmos* bearing so directly on this view, that
though it will probably have presented itself to the
reader's mind, he may thank me for reproducing it.
" If we imagine, as in a vision of fancy, the acute-
ness of our senses preturnaturally sharpened even to
the extreme limit of telescopic vision, and incidents
which are separated by vast intervals of time compressed into a day or an hour, everything like rest
in spacial existence will forthwith disappear. We
shall find the innumerable host of the fixed stars
commoved in groups in different directions; nebulæ
drawing hither and thither like cosmic clouds; our
milky way breaking up in particular parts, and its
veil rent. Motion in every point of the vault of
heaven, as on the surface of the earth, in the germi-

nating, leaf-pushing, flower-unfolding organisms of its vegetable covering. The celebrated Spanish botanist, Cavanilles, first conceived the thought of ' seeing grass grow' by setting the horizontal thread of a micrometer, attached to a powerful telescope, at one time upon the tip of the shoot of a bamboo, at another upon that of a fast-growing American aloe (*Agave Americana*), precisely as the astronomer brings a culminating star upon the cross-wires of his instrument. In the aggregate life of nature, organic as well as sidereal, Being, Maintaining, and Becoming are alike associated with motion."

Here we will pause, and abstain from argument. Let the thought stand as a suggestion merely, a whim of fantasy. It is at least a noble and elevating one. The dissevered unity of nature is restored. The lower rises to the higher rank; the higher wins a new glory in descending to the lower place. Unbroken stands the scheme before us. Life infinite and boundless; throbbing in our veins with a tiny thrill of the vast pulse that courses through the infinitude of space; the joy and sorrow in our hearts calling us to an universal sympathy, guaranteeing to us a sympathy that is universal, in return.

The subjects we have discussed might almost be regarded as riddles, presented to us by a Higher Intelligence, in order to cultivate the powers that are exercised in solving them. Nor can this thought be otherwise than welcome to us. Surely man is but a child. I am "an infant crying in the night," says the sweet poet of the modern time, and the words find an echo in all hearts, because they are true of all humanity. Man is a little child, and as a little child he is taught. His feeble powers are drawn gently out, in tender sportive ways. Lord Bacon says, in words which prove in him a sensibility of heart as exquisite as the reach of his intellect was sublime: "Of the sciences which contemplate nature, the sacred philosopher pronounces, 'It is the glory of God to conceal a thing: but the glory of the king to search it out:' not otherwise than as if the Divine Nature delighted in the innocent and kindly play of children, who hide themselves in order that they may be found, and in his indulgent goodness towards mankind, had chosen for

His playfellow the human soul." Nature sports with
us, presenting to us easy questions in hard ways.
She gives us riddles—the fact simple, the mode in
which it is put before us complicated and involved.
We think in every possible wrong way, before we
find the right; but in the meantime our faculties are
strengthened and enlarged. Our chief difficulty in
comprehending Nature is her simplicity, the multitude and boundless variety of results which she
educes from one law, and this law, it may be, self-
evident and impossible not to be. We cannot, till
we have learnt by long experience, understand what
great events from simple causes spring, nor how
truly "the workmanship of God is such that He
doth hang the greatest weight upon the smallest
wires."

How amazing it is to trace the wonderful processes of life, even so partially and feebly as we have
done, to the simplest laws of force. And yet more
amazing is it, to reflect that these same laws extend
illimitably over the field of nature. If they bear
such fruit in one least corner of the universe—for
"if a man meditate upon the universal frame of

nature, what is the earth but a little heap of dust?"—
in what rich harvests of order, beauty, life, may they
not issue, through all the immeasurable sphere of
their dominion! Before the resources of creative
power, imagination stands silent and appalled.

The study of Nature, revealing to us, though
faintly, yet truly, traces of the laws and methods
of the Highest and Universal Worker—revealing
to us, in His work, an absolute singleness of aim
and unity of means, perfectness of calm repose one
with unfailing energy of action—this study has its
worthy end, only when it raises us to act like Him:
with steadfast and single aim which no passion can
pervert, nor interest corrupt; with means which,
ever changing, are yet ever one in changeless rec-
titude; with an activity untiring, and a calmness
that cannot be disturbed, rooted in love and trust.

CHAPTER VII.

THE LIVING WORLD.

THIS course of thought became the starting point, in my own mind, of a further train of reflections, which took a wider sweep, and which seem to me to conduct to results of great importance. Let me beg the reader to accompany me a short distance in pursuing it. If our former arguments are sound, the result at which we arrive is this—that not only are the organic and inorganic worlds, which seem to be so different, truly one, exhibiting the same forces, powers, and laws; but life itself, or that which we have called so, appears as a mere result of chemical and mechanical agencies, into the effects of which its most distinctive phenomena are resolved. We find no special power which we can call by that name.

May it not, then, be urged that we have grasped at life, and it has escaped us? Those processes which we find in its place are not what we sought—are not what we can recognize. Life on this view is not explained; it is denied. It is true that it is made universal, but in that very universality the thing itself is lost. The passive processes which are substituted for it present not one of the characters which we seem to feel and know in life—fulfil not one of our instinctive affirmations respecting it. Have we not analyzed it into nonentity?—found the fair seeming fruit to be but ashes?

In a certain sense I feel that this is true. By life we do not mean, and we cannot accept as its explanation, any mere results of material laws. Our souls may be over-ridden by demonstrations to this effect, silenced by evidence to which we may not deny assent, but they are not satisfied. There is another life than an aggregate of material processes: whatever may be the appearance, *that* cannot be the truth. Life is a unity, not a group of results; a power, not a mere effect.

These thoughts, and others to which I shall refer

presently, worked in my mind. I could not be blind to what seemed to me plain and indubitable facts—facts which showed that the most characteristic phenomena ascribed to life had their source in chemical activities and mechanical conditions. I could not wish to be blind to them; for they seemed to me to possess an exquisite beauty, and to give an invaluable simplicity and definiteness to our conceptions. They seemed right, true, delightful; yet there was in them something that was not right. They made Nature less, or seemed to make it so.

And this also one could not but feel:—How should it be that the investigation of life, above all other studies, should have such an insidious tendency to conduct to results which the heart repudiates? Why should that study especially, though pursued with the best aims and hopes, lead us, alike unwittingly and unwillingly, to results which seemed, at least to some, hostile to religion, threatening to man's best hopes? Why were our enthusiastic pursuit of those glimmerings of light which it were false to our Maker not to pursue, our glad grasp of some clear signs of order and necessity in this dark-seeming corner of Nature, destined to lead us to mere blank and void? Surely there must have been some misapprehension here—some latent false thought, the effects of which were thus made manifest.

Nor, indeed, were these feelings long in finding satisfaction. Through the fresh light which I had gained respecting Life, my eyes were opened to perceive the meaning of some other facts, which until then had possessed for me but little significance. In common with the rest of thinking people, I had often heard the doctrine stated that we know only phenomena.* I had considered more or less the grounds on which this was affirmed, and I suppose that the passive condition of my mind in respect to it represented pretty well that of the majority of men. But when I obtained these views of Life, this doctrine rose from a mere speculation into a practical truth. It became a new possession to me; for I could not but recognize in it the key to the

---

* For the proofs on which this doctrine is based, reference may be made to the writings of Sir W. Hamilton ; or especially to the able summary recently given in Mr. H. Spencer's *First Principles*.

strife in which I found myself engaged.   If those
things which we call the physical world — the
substances and forces with which Science deals—
are but phenomenal (that is, if they are but appearances of some existence which we thus perceive
not as it is), then the reducing of physical life to
the results of chemical and mechanical processes no
more disappoints the intellect, or makes a discord
in the soul.

Life is not thereby banished from the world: it
is but shown to have its seat in that which is not
phenomenal.   It is a living world which we thus
perceive under the appearance of passive forces;
of chemistry and mechanism.   The authority of our
native instincts, the trustworthiness of our deepest
feelings, are still maintained; they are restored with
fuller sway.   Of the two results that seem to follow
from the scientific investigation of life—the universality of its presence, and its resolution into dead
mechanic force — the former remains a truth, the
latter is but an appearance.   Life *is* universal: it
only *seems* to be mechanical.

See! we give up, at the call of truth, what we

desire and love; and in the end we receive it back, increased a thousandfold.   Laid in the ground and *dying*, the seed bears much fruit.

I say, the authority of our instincts and emotions with respect to Life is restored, and more than restored.   They rise into a liberty which could hardly have been conceived before; for, in truth, all investigation into the laws of the material world, and the discovery of the undisturbed dominion of those laws in the organic kingdom, is but the casting off of the shackles which constrain and bind them down.   We cannot think worthily of Life, until we see that it is not in these physical things at all, which possess but the shadows and appearances of it; till we carry our thoughts beyond.   For which deliverance the needful condition is that our false thought of Life, as an agent having its seat in the few poor things that we call living, should be wholly set aside.   When we are freed from that persuasion our minds can rise up and walk; the palsy of our limbs is cured.

There is no such life as that which thus there seems.   There cannot be.   The conception of such

an acting or regulating power in the physical world
carries a contradiction in itself. The physical is
the sphere of passive results; its order is a mere
sequence of effects; as being phenomenal, indeed,
it is necessarily so. Life is higher than that fancied
power embodied in organic things; or there is none.
And the problem which we have to answer is plain:
it is to find *that* Life, of which the seeming life
in the organic world, the seeming deadness in the
inorganic, alike are the appearance. Nor can we
hesitate as to the means by which the solution
of this problem is to be attempted. Our higher
instincts, our loftier feelings, exist for this end.
They demand of us to rise above the physical;
they are violated and crushed when we bring them
down within its cruel gripe; their very nature
proclaims their native sphere to be in that which
the phenomenal does not include. They derive
their existence thence, and must be its interpreters.

And being set free by the knowledge that the
physical world with all its laws and forces is but
an appearance, how perfectly adapted they show
themselves for the work on which we demand their

service. To picture to ourselves, to apprehend, the very Life, the living world, which appears to us under these mechanic forms, this is what we need their aid to do. It is a world that must surpass in depth and fulness this world of mere phenomena; a world in which Life truly dwells, as it does not in this; a world of action, in the true sense of the term, as this is not; a world of perfect order, which the beautiful (yet, alas! how often cold and cruel) passive order of this world reflects: and we have hearts and souls to know it by.

What is it that appears to us under the phenomena which we know as those of Life, regarded at once in their results and in their law? This is the question we must ask. We find it easy to invent an imaginary power, such as " the vital principle," which might (as we suppose) effect all the marvellous results of use and adaptation in the organic world, itself being exempted from the dominion of the common laws, and operating simply to those ends. But our true problem is a higher one than this, and admits not of such hasty answer. It taxes more than the imagination, and cannot be met by words which express no meaning. For it is nothing less than this (and the awe with which the thought impressed me first is present to me still), what is the true significance of that law, which, appearing to us under the simple form that motion takes the direction of least resistance (a mere definition, mere truism as it is), yet brings forth the varied order, the beauty and adaptations, the ends and uses full of manifest love, which the animated world reveals? What is this law of least resistance — of seeming physical necessity—which bears such fruits? What fact is it that shines through this " phenomenon ? "

In order to feel the question aright, we need to retain both terms of the problem well in our thoughts. There are the *results* of life on the one hand; there is the necessary law embodied in it, on the other. The true thought of life must account for not only one, but both. In life there is a necessity which seems mechanical; there is a result which is divine. How shall we read this riddle?

I had not long pondered this problem, when I felt that it raised itself out of the intellectual into the moral sphere; and that, in truth, it was a spiritual fact that thus presented itself to us under a material guise. Translated from its passive phenomenal form into the terms of true action, this law of least resistance assumes a moral meaning: it expresses rightness—love. It is adapted, thus, to bear the fruits we see it yield.

In dealing thus with Life, holding it with both hands, as it were, looking at it on both its sides— its law and its results—and so binding ourselves by the true conditions of the problem; and remembering also that nature is not truly what it is to our apprehensions, but is something more; we are forced to feel that the phenomena of organic life put us in the presence of a spiritual fact. And since in that life there is nothing more than is throughout all nature, nature itself must be the phenomenon— or appearance—of the spiritual world.

To this point I was brought, and feel myself still inevitably brought, by the studies to which the science of physiology committed me. If there be any life in nature—and how can we deny it?—it is a spiritual life. For in nature regarded as material there is none ; nothing but dead and passive laws bearing incredible fruits ; apparently effecting in their blind working results which express to us not only life, but love !

But these very laws themselves, sublime in their simplicity, carry their own claim to be held spiritual : they speak distinctly to our hearts of that which is not physical, but is kindred to the soul. For in thinking of this law of least resistance to which we have seen reason to believe organic forms are to be referred, how could I help perceiving such things as these ? First, that, rightly speaking, it is hardly to be called a law at all : it is simply the nature and necessity of things. Motion, as we have seen, can take no direction but that of least resistance : regarding the proposition in its most general form, it is less a " law " of motion than its nature. And, therefore, in the very constitution of the world, we perceive with an awful wonder that there are involved all the results of form and structure that are realized in living things. It is the exhibition to us of a fact to which, by its very nature, these results belon g.

And if, again (calling our moral nature to aid and carry up our intellectual apprehension), we look at this law to which we have traced the living structure, and endeavour to realize its significance, we feel that it is a spiritual fact with which we are in relation. Interpreted into moral terms, is not the law of least resistance this, *Action determined by want; giving, called into operation by a need?* Is not this " appearance," this disguise of a material law, worthy to present to us a fact of which the verity is love? It is love that appears to us under this seeming law of force; love not less demonstrated in its nature, than made manifest in its fruits.

Thus was first suggested to me a thought I have elsewhere pursued at greater length,* that this physical world, known to be an appearance (or phenomenon,) is the appearance of that spiritual world which we also know. It is not the phenomenon of a merely unknown existence therefore; but of that " spiritual" which has a moral nature,

---

* See *Man and his Dwelling-Place*, book i. chap. ii., *et seq.*

with which we associate the thoughts of love, of righteousness, of true necessity. The facts which life presents to us, when seen with the eyes of science, assert for themselves this character. We have to do with a spiritual fact in that necessity which makes living things what they are.

But this necessity is the same as that by which the rest of nature is what it is. The same law or necessity of force which determines the former, determines all. We learn better from the organic as it is nearer us; we see nature more truly there where it is less beyond our scope. And thus I seemed to be taught that the essential fact which all things imperfectly exhibit to us is spiritual also, and fraught with moral elements.

The appeal lies here to the heart: and, surely, it gives no equivocal reply. As plainly as facts can speak to the moral nature, does this fact of the union of perfect law and beneficent result, of a necessity so inherent in the nature of the case, and fruits which a moral necessity alone could involve, speak of a spiritual essence in that which we call nature.

And then I could not but feel, too, what confirmation this thought receives from the light it introduces into our experience. When I bethought myself, again, what Nature is to us; what sensations connect us with it, what emotions gather round it; the conviction became overwhelming. It is the spiritual world that thus impresses us; that gives us an experience thus altogether above, and inexplicable by, the powers we can attribute to these phenomenal things. Viewed as the appearance of the spiritual, Nature becomes intelligible: Life, which science seemed to banish, returns to it; its mysterious capacity to move us receives its explanation; the powers of the soul find it a fitting sphere for their exercise, and prove their claim to be its best interpreters.

All which comes from the doctrine, established so long in the region of philosophy, yet barren till vivified by union with science, that the physical or material Nature, which we know, is but an appearance of a true Nature which is more than it.

CHAPTER VIII.

NATURE AND MAN.

THUS I saw the value there is in the doctrine that
Nature is more than it appears to us; a doctrine carefully elaborated and established by the arguments of a
long succession of thinkers, and yet turned to so little
use. It seemed to me like a weapon carefully wrought
and keenly tempered, but the edge of which had not
been tried: or like the splendid geometry of the
Greeks, upon which a large part of modern science is
built as its corner stone, but which its authors
applied to no practical result. I saw especially how
needful it was for the right understanding of scientific
truths, and how perfectly it put at rest the strife
which science has waged, more or less continuously,
with the religion and with the higher emotions of the
race.

For I perceived that while on the one hand we possess instinctive feelings which bind us consciously to nature as it truly is, on the other hand science is ever bringing more clearly into our consciousness what nature is to our apprehension, which falls short of this; it is continually bringing the phenomenal (or apparent) into clearer light, and forcing upon us thereby the contrast between that, and those feelings of ours which go beyond it. There could not fail to be such a result from the prosecution of the task which science sets herself. Instinctive feelings of ours, true, more or less perfectly, to nature as it is (as, for example, the feeling that there is life in it), are attached by us to the merely phenomenal, and this is done without perception of the discord so long as we remain ignorant. But science, showing us the phenomena more and more accurately, bringing out clearly what the seeming order of nature is, necessarily seems to oppose and deny these feelings.

Our heart, in a word, asserts the true; science reveals to us the apparent. This sums up and solves the long-standing controversy between them; it is strange if it do not make the parties to it the best of

friends and mutual servitors, each supplying to the
other what most it needs. And this result we owe—
it should be remembered for their sakes and our own
—to the labours of those men who have proved by
long and patient demonstration that the things which
answer to our apprehension of nature are but an
appearance of it; men who have often seemed to be
labouring in the obscurest and most abstract regions,
often to little or no purpose, from whose pursuits the
sympathy of the world has been often entirely with-
held; yet who by a divine instinct would not cease
their toil, nor divert it to more inviting paths. We
can see now, reaping the fruit of their labours, why
they persevered. For, as so many times has been
the case, the loftiest and most abstruse work becomes
in its results the most universal, practical, and simple.
So, for example, the prosecution of the highest
mathematics has added to the intellectual possessions
of the child, and serves to guide the least instructed
sailor. And so, too, the arduous attempt to fathom
the nature of things, and penetrate the conditions of
our knowledge, has furnished a basis from which the
most childlike heart may look with fresh eyes upon

the world, and the most simple find his path made clearer. For each man may know and be assured not only that he may, but that he must, regard the facts of his own and others' history, the events of his and their experience, as being something more and other than that which he perceives in them, and may call in with confidence his best and highest feelings to guide him in his belief what this must be.

And not only so ; it seemed to me we might go farther, and from the study of nature obtain a deeper knowledge respecting man. When I gained the perception that nature must be regarded as universally living, I could not help asking why it was not so perceived by us. How comes there to be that appearance of deadness in the universe which makes the organic world seem so distinctively endowed with life, and which has prompted the familiar term "dead matter?" If nature is living, why do we perceive it dead?

Pondering this question, there grew upon me the thought that its solution was to be found in a change of our idea respecting man. If there be a deadness perceived in nature, when it is not there, may not this be because there is a deadness, unsuspected by himself, in man? May not a want of life of his own be thus reflected on him from without? It was thus the first thought of a deadness in man was suggested to me. How could it be escaped? Can any one escape it who fairly meets the evidence that universal nature is the seat of life, and then reflects that he calls it—and perceives it as if it were—" dead matter ? "

Nay, can any one wish to escape it who suffers himself to dwell on the conception, and tries to appreciate its meaning? I cannot believe it ; to me the evidence seems too powerful, the results too consolatory. For by just as much as we lower our present estimate of man's perfection, by so much is our thought of that which surrounds him elevated ; by so much is our anticipation of his future aggrandized. To deny that his life is wanting is to bind him down to the cruel present ; to affirm it is to rise, in belief, in hope, in energy. What he now is ceases to be a standard by which his hopes should be bounded or his circumstances judged. And then again can we forget the many voices, not only human, but divine, by which this thought of man's present state has found utterance? Driven, by studies which were of nature alone, to the conception of a deadness that had invaded man, and marred his feeling, could I fail to recognize anew, and with a solemn gladness, the truthfulness of words in which the Bible speaks of man, and which affirm so unequivocally, so centrally, his want of life? Must I not have been glad to find that science spoke one language with that book?

Nor with that book only, but with the utterances of men who had never known it. I could not but recall how many times, in ancient literature, the thought had been expressed that this seeming life of ours surely was not, could not be, the Life of Man. Of these utterances it is sufficient to quote the words which Cicero puts into the mouth of Africanus: "Yea, they live who have fled from the bonds of the body as from a dungeon; but your life, as it is called, is death."*

---

* "Immo vero, inquit, ii vivunt qui ex corporum vinculis, tanquam e carcere evolaverunt; vestra vero quæ dicitur vita, mors est."— *Somnium Scipionis.*

These expressions also seem to have been associated in the minds of those who used them with a
more or less distinct belief in the universal life of
nature. And thus I perceived again how this
ancient doctrine of nature's life is restored, in
union with all the advances made by science, which
for a time has seemed to put it aside. The distinction we have been taught to make between nature
as it truly is, and our apprehension of it through its
phenomena, gives us this thought again, raised, as
we have seen, to a higher significance, as affirming
now not a material but a spiritual life.

And so I was led also to a more distinct thought
in reference to the deadness I seemed to recognize in
man. It was a spiritual deadness. The very fact of
which the Scriptures speak seem to be proclaimed by
science. A want of life that is spiritual appeared
to me the demonstrable clue to our present experience, and thus a fact essentially religious, and of
the highest religious worth, seemed to find an unex-
pected proof.

And thus, too, a new apprehension arose in me
concerning the nature of the spiritual life itself and

the meaning of its absence. I perceived that it was
a deeper and more fruitful thing than I had supposed
it; that man's spiritual life, or want of it, was a fact
which had consequences, and manifested itself in
results, that had not been suspected; which went
deep into the essence of our being, and determined
our whole experience.

Not that I supposed the New Testament to mean
by that which it terms man's " death," any mode of
our perceiving nature. But it seemed to me most
reasonable, when once the fact had presented itself to
my thoughts, that spiritual life (which is surely the
truest and most essential life of man), or the want of
it (which is surely his deepest and most absolute
want), should express themselves in our experience
in ways which ought to become manifest to us when
that experience was rigorously studied; and that the
mode in which we perceive nature, feeling a deadness when deadness is not there, was one effect which
might well ensue.

Here, however, I felt a difficulty. No change in
a man's spiritual or moral state affects his mode of
perceiving nature. This is most true. We must

carry our thoughts, here, alike beyond moral changes
and individual men. The spiritual state is not the
moral condition merely: it is that essential being
from which the moral condition flows. And man's
deadness is not an individual thing, nor to be
removed by individual change; it has a wider
sphere, embracing all humanity, and a wider remedy
embracing also all humanity. So we find, in the
language of St. Paul, a clear distinction drawn
between the life of which he had already become
the recipient, and the perfect life for which he
hoped. According to his words, salvation may be
ours now; yet we look also for a salvation more
complete hereafter.

If, then, this state of ours do not exhibit it, what
is the true Life of Man? We have some means of
answering this question. In all times and in all
places men have looked forward to a different and
better state of being. Under various forms the idea
has ever been present to their thought and to their
hope: it is emphatically present to our own. It
appeared to me, as my thoughts respecting life
unfolded themselves, that the time had come when

12

this idea of a better state of being might assume a more definite meaning.

It is a moral change—the deliverance from corruption—which we are conscious of needing most; which all who are raised above the lowest most earnestly desire. But in no man's thought of heaven does the idea of a moral change stand alone. We need more. There must be a change also in our being—a deliverance or a gain affecting the mode of our existence. Guided by the thoughts I have mentioned, I felt that these two ideas united themselves into one, or at least sprang from one root, and found their full expression in the idea of a perfected life.

For this perfected life, giving us the perception of Nature as it is—as spiritual—and bringing us into conscious relation not with the changing phenomena alone (as now we seem to be), but with the essential existence, the same in all and unaffected by their changes, must involve a moral difference in us too. Our relations being widened so, our interests could no more revolve about our self, our passions be no more perverted. The possibility of evil or of temptation to it, as now we feel them, would be gone. The truer and profounder consciousness would obliterate them for ever; the larger and intenser life swallow them up in good; making what now we call loss to be no loss, and sacrifice to be possession. Thus heaven is the Life of Man. Perfect deliverance from evil is in perfect Life.

CHAPTER IX.

THE PHENOMENAL AND THE TRUE.

IDEAS of this order were irresistibly forced on me
by my studies in physiology, of which they seem,
indeed, to me to be the necessary consequence. We
cannot divide our nature into two portions, and say,
This belongs to science, this to religion. No such
barrier exists; the attempt to erect one inevitably
fails. The study of physical objects *is* the study of
that which is most profoundly spiritual, and must
be recognized as being so, if it is to be carried on
freely, fully, or to any satisfactory result. Questions
relating to our spiritual nature, if not deliberately
faced and solved, are sure, consciously or unconsciously, to embarrass all our inquiries: rightly
solved, they seem to me to give as great a liberty
and vantage-ground to thought, as they impose

bondage upon it if they are avoided or falsely conceived.   Accepting the idea of a deadness in Man, and a true or spiritual life in Nature, new sources of light opened upon me, and my path seemed to grow clear in almost all directions.

And I have thus briefly indicated the line of thought which led me to it, because I find it at once the fruit and the seed of the scientific know-ledge of Nature.   Even a slight understanding of the true order of physical phenomena, and of the significance of the physical laws, is sufficient to conduct us to it; from that point it becomes our guide.   I shall therefore endeavour to place it in a little clearer light.

The assertion that our knowledge or perception is not of the essence of things, but of something merely phenomenal or relative, translated into more ordinary language, means that we are feeling things to exist which do not exist.*

---

* Thus, to illustrate the proposition, Kant takes a rose, and says of it—" The rose is not a thing in itself, but a mere phenomenon." But it is evidently the rose and nothing else that we feel as the thing.

Now, strange as this may seem when thus generally stated, there is nothing we can better understand, when it is expressed in matter-of-fact terms,
and applied to particular cases. "We are feeling
things to be which are not; our practically true is
not the very truth." There is not the least difficulty in this: our practically true in any large
matter is continually not the true. Is not the earth
practically flat? Or again: it is the established
doctrine of science, proved by overwhelming evidence, that motion, once begun, never comes to an
end: the world is what it is because all the motion
within it never ceases. Yet, practically, motion
continually ceases: we have *consciously* to do with
motions that, for the most part, come to a speedy
end. Thus an unceasing motion gives us the feeling
and the perception of ceasing motions; and the
round earth gives us the feeling and perception of a
flat one.

Our "practical," therefore, may not be the true in
any case. In fact, it is evident that in any case in
which we are relatively very small, and our powers
are capable of apprehending very partially, it cer-

tainly will not be the true.   It is not hard, therefore, to credit that our practical world altogether (this world of " things," as we perceive it, or of " matter and force," as science represents it) is not the truly existing one; but is only the inadequate impression we receive from a world of a different order.   It is a question of our capacity to perceive.

But there are other illustrations which may serve to make this idea still more intelligible.   We may easily perceive how, not only a partial, but a universal feeling of the existence of that which does not exist might arise.   Let us conceive, for example, the case of a person in whom the sense of *touch* was wanting—that is, who could see things naturally, but had not the power of feeling.   It is clear that, by such a person, the appearances of things (which we and all who have their senses perfect feel and know to be but appearances) would be felt as having real and separate existence.   He would have no faculty by which to test them and discover their true nature, not having any apprehension of that solid thing of which they were the appearances.   Seeing a book or a chair, for example, in various positions, before his eyes, he would consciously perceive, not several appearances of one book or chair, but so many distinct things,—realities, existences practically to him, because filling all his faculties, and exhausting the scope of his (maimed and mutilated) powers.

Let us observe well the point here: the deficiency of a faculty which belongs to our nature would elevate what are in truth mere appearances into a *felt* reality; would give them, to our feeling, a fictitious existence which they do not possess. On the other hand, the imparting to such a person (so feeling mere appearances to be realities) the use of his full powers—the giving back to him the sense of touch—would reduce these appearances again, in respect to his feeling, to their right position. From their false reality they would sink back into the mere appearances they are. And this by no loss, but simply by a gain to him.

Thus we see how the absence of a faculty is adapted to give us a feeling of reality in respect to that which does not exist:—in the case supposed, it would make that seem *real* which is but *appearance*. The same fact is presented to us in another form in the case (no more a mere hypothesis) of dreaming. In dreams, non-existent things are felt as if existing; we live, to our feeling, a life which is not lived, and amid conditions which are not. And this we do simply through the temporary abeyance or inaction of certain of our faculties. For this is the essential difference between dreaming and imagining. The very same thoughts which constitute a dream might pass through the waking mind in felt unreality, and constitute a poem or a tale. But some of our faculties are inoperative during sleep (the power of the will, and probably some others); there is a temporary absence of their action; and, as a consequence, existence is felt as pertaining to that which does not exist.

If, therefore, in our experience of material things we are feeling that to exist to which existence does not truly belong, the fact is capable of the simplest explanation: it implies merely the absence or comparative inactivity of some faculty in us; of some faculty belonging to our perfect nature. It is the known effect of such a cause to give a false feeling of existence.

And, therefore, when it is said that we do not know that which actually exists; that we cannot penetrate to the essence of Nature, and must be content with its appearances; we may readily understand both what the fact is and its consequence. A faculty that belongs to our perfect nature is wanting in us, or is imperfectly in action: that we have a false feeling of existence in respect to that which is truly but an appearance (the physical world), is an inevitable effect of this.

Thus we are brought by another path to the idea of a deadness as involved in our present state. It is exhibited to us from another side. We have found that thought forced upon us by the seeming deadness of almost the whole of Nature, and the banishing of life, by our investigation, even from that part in which it seemed to dwell. Now we perceive evidence that, in respect to us, the deepest and most essential powers of manhood are in abeyance. Do not these two views mutually interpret and confirm each other? Man's want of life expresses itself thus.

And a further light is cast also upon that life itself. It would be perfected in us by the perfect bestowal of the powers that are wanting now : in a perfect consciousness, that is ; a perfect apprehension of that which truly is.   To possess that were to be consciously in the spiritual world ; and that were to live, in the truest sense of living.

But farther, this conception of our state, as I have said, is a guide to our thoughts of Nature.   One consequence that follows from it is this : that we do not apply the idea of true existence to the world we practically have to do with (this world of material things); we recognize that that idea is applicable only to another.   We recognize that our idea of existence (as well as our emotions and instinctive feelings) goes beyond this world which we consciously perceive, and belongs to that alone of which this is the appearance.   When we think, therefore, of these things which are practically to us, we do not ask how they can *be*, but only how they can appear.   We abstain from testing them by the idea of true existence.   How can this *appear?* and what is it which thus appears ?—these are our questions : not what *is* this? or, by what means can it *be?*

Thus almost every problem we can encounter is

greatly simplified; every question is made easier by all the difference there is between existing and seeming to exist. And a division is made for us beforehand of all inquiries that can arise—a division which more than halves their difficulty. How should this appear? or, what is this appearance? we ask, on the one hand; and, on the other, why do we feel it not only to appear, but to exist?—of which the latter is ever answered for us ere we ask it.

CHAPTER X.

FORCE.

WE may endeavour to cast a glance on some of the subjects which thus open themselves out before us, and briefly note how the phenomena of the physical world present themselves as a book to be read by the light of our moral and emotional nature. First among these subjects stands Force.

We are familiar enough by our own experience with the idea which this word conveys. We use force whenever we effect any motion of ourselves or other things; we feel it as acting on us when we are moved. Naturally from this basis we extend the idea into the whole series of physical events, and conceive a force as operating in every change which takes place around us. But in this natural idea we are not suffered to remain. It is true we feel force, and cannot but feel it, when we are conscious of exerting ourselves either for action or resistance; but also, almost whenever we are conscious at all, we feel *sensations*—of pleasure, pain, light, sound, or taste, and so on. Yet, though feeling these, we do not infer the existence of such sensations in nature. They are our own merely; only the child fancies his pleasure or pain to be also in the things that impart it to him. But that which the child does in ascribing his feeling of pain to the insensitive table, we do in ascribing our feeling of force, which is really that of exertion, to the material world. Force can no more be separated from a perceiving consciousness, such as our own, than colour or sweetness. We are called on to recognize here, as we have already done in respect to other sensations, that our own nature contributes to them, and that our feeling is not the standard of what is without us, but the effect produced upon ourselves.

Now it is, doubtless, difficult to do this in respect to force, and to admit that it is not (as we feel it to be) in the very objects that seem to exert it. The difficulty is shown by the fact that the question still needs to be argued, and that the mass of men would be at issue with the thinkers respecting it. But from the point of view we have taken, at once the truth of the statement, and the source of the difficulty in receiving it, become obvious. If that which only appears is felt by us as existing, our feeling of force where it is not is an evident conseqence. In truth, this feeling of force in nature is the very expression of the fact of our feeling as existing that which does not exist. It is rather that very feeling itself; for it presents to us objects as at once passive and yet acting—as without power, and yet exerting power. It is, indeed, precisely in consequence of this feeling of force, and the merely mechanical character which belongs to it, that men have ascribed deadness to nature, and spoken of it as "dead matter." The acceptance of force as arising only within our own feeling is the conceding a spiritual existence to that which is without. Thus the persuasion that force is in nature cannot be really given up, but with the admission of an untruthfulness in our feeling of existence. The two things are in-

separably joined.   Physical objects exert force as
truly as they exist; and they do both alike only to
our feeling.

So in accepting that thought of man's condition
which involves such a mode of feeling on our part
as its result, this difficulty respecting force, which
else meets us on the threshold of our inquiries, is
cleared away.   The feeling of force where it is not
is implied beforehand in what we have already
learnt of ourselves and nature.

And so we may advance unimpeded to other
results, which are of the greatest scientific import.
If the physical world is the changing appearance of
some unchanging existence, there must be in it a
perfect order through all its changes, and an essential identity at all times.   The force apparent in it,
therefore, will be at all times equivalent.   It will
change its forms, but never vary in itself; it may
become hidden, but it cannot cease.   That necessity
of order which belongs to an appearance necessitates
this.   There cannot be true variation, because an
appearance cannot change itself.

Thus, not only is the apparent merging of each

form of force—motion, heat, light, affinity, &c.—in each other, with no loss or gain, a necessary part of the order of phenomena,* but another character of force, which is involved in this, is also seen to be necessary, and to be full of a significance of its own.

For, if the amount of force is always the same, and every process in which it is concerned is a change merely of its form or place, then every such process must have two aspects: on the one side force comes into play ; on the other, to an exactly equal amount, it ceases. Its operation is always and inevitably an equal plus and minus. There cannot be the one without the other. Every physical process is, necessarily, the adding of force in one direction, the withdrawing it in the opposite, and may be represented by the equivalent, but opposed, motions of the two sides of a balance. This we have seen to be the case in respect to the

---

* For the discussion of this subject the reader is referred to Mr. Grove's admirable treatise on the Correlation of the Physical Forces ; it has been briefly treated by the writer in the *Cornhill Magazine* for October, 1861.

organic world. Organic life, taken as a whole, presents itself to the eye of science as a vibration. It
is summed up in opposite and equal processes. And
this idea applies equally to the whole sphere of
physical events. However varied, however vast,
however minute, may be the changes which mark
the course of nature, they all have this character.
Nature vibrates, with perpetual plus and minus; it
vibrates, and no more. What music it thus makes
in the ear of Omnipotence, into what vast sym-
phony its endless, unintermitting, infinitely-varied
pulsings may be wrought, we know not. It is
enough that the Great Musician knows. But this
we cannot fail to note: that be it wrought into whatsoever forms, spread out over whatsoever time, equal
plus and minus are—nonentity. An 0, analysed
and spread out, and made to seem to be. This is
what the physical world avows itself to the long-
gazing, and at last penetrating eye of man. So
much to him, so much in seeming, is it truly nothing
then—a painted vision, and no more? Must we
mourn the loss, the utter sinking away of our
imaginary world into a false play of illusions?

It is not so. Already we have known, and have rejoiced to know, that nature, as we perceive it, is but a vision; for it is a vision presented to our eye by that which is infinitely more. This inverted telescope of science which dissipates the galaxies and dissolves the stars, reducing nature into nothingness, strikes us with no astonishment, fills us with no dismay. This solid-seeming universe may fade before its gaze; it does but bring us into a surer presence of the things that are unseen.

CHAPTER XI.

THE ORGANIC AND THE INORGANIC.

IF the ideas we have been considering in respect
to organic life are true, we cannot but feel that, to a
certain extent, our former thoughts have been
inverted.   We have long been accustomed to hear it
assumed, that the organic world is distinguished at
once by a special eminence over the rest of nature,
and by a special mystery; so that it is that which of
all things we can least hope to understand.   It
seems to me, however, that this idea is the very
opposite of the truth.   So far from being less com-
prehensible than the rest of nature, the organic world
appears rather to be that very part of it which we
may most truly be said to know: the inorganic world
with its deep-hidden forces is the mystery.   For it

must not be forgotten that, in discussing organic life, we pre-suppose the chemical affinities; and these being taken as our postulates, the phenomena of the organic world are of the kind which we best understand. As based on an opposition, by other forces, to those chemical affinities, and as displaying powers due to the force thus stored up, life presents to us no mystery. Almost we might say that it exhibits to us, under this aspect, the one thing in respect to the natural forces that we may be said to comprehend: the production of a tension and its results. And remembering the effect exerted by the forces of nature in maintaining and increasing this tension, and by mechanical conditions in moulding the material so produced; remembering these things, we can hardly call life mysterious at all. It presents to us a lively instance of known, and, in one sense, well-understood phenomena. But there is a mystery in it, doubtless. In making us conscious of the presence of a mystery it has done us good service, though our wonder has been misplaced. The organic life we understand; but those wider forces and affinities which underlie it, and by virtue of which alone it can exist, contain a yet unpenetrated secret. It is to these we should turn our admiration and devote our curiosity. All the activity we see in the organic world is derived from them; from them are borrowed all the complex structure and mutual adaptations it displays. We have magnified the little and despised the great.

And naturally we have done so; for, in truth, this feeling of ours respecting the organic and inorganic worlds is a legitimate fruit of our ignorance. Where we have known least we have seen least, and have felt least wonder. Our ignorance where most profound has been least visible to ourselves. This poor organic life, being, as it were, our own, being the part of nature nearest to us, least above us—being, perhaps we might say, the part of nature which is brought down within the sphere of our appreciation —this we have seen truly enough to perceive its wonder; knowing it better we have regarded it with a peculiar awe, and have arrogated to it a peculiar value. The inorganic world being larger, on a grander scale, and devoted to ends less fathomable by our ingenuity, this we have not known well

enough even to discover that we do not know it.   It
has seemed less to us because farther from our eye;
more simple because our vision could not trace it.
We have seen life no farther than the life that is
like our own extends.

In another form we may perceive a similar result
of our limited apprehension of nature; namely, in
our belief that consciousness is confined to the
animal creation and mysteriously associated with one
portion alone of their physical structure.   Perceiving
all nature as unconscious, save ourselves, and creatures organized like ourselves, we assume that nature
is an unconscious thing, and that here and there
a little consciousness is imported into it from without.
But what are the facts?   At one small corner of
nature we perceive it (we may say) directly, we are
in immediate contact with it—namely, in our brain:
and there we feel it as conscious.   At every other
point we perceive it only indirectly, through chan-
nels which hide as well as reveal; and there it
appears unconscious; or conscious only by inference,
from resemblance to ourselves.   Where man and
nature touch, he feels nature to be not only the pos-

sessor of consciousness, but the reservoir, the holder,
of his own.   Where he is parted from it, and obtains
his apprehension of it through senses which present
it partially and at second hand, the consciousness is
wanting; he apprehends brute matter only.

Is not the true interpretation of these facts obvious
when we reflect on them, once freeing ourselves from
the natural assumption into which our limited feeling has betrayed us ?   Is it not this : that nature is
a conscious existence, and that the apparent absence
of consciousness from it arises from our non-percep-
tion?   Just as a conversation, rich with love and
wisdom, heard at a distance, becomes to us mere
sound.

And thus we return to our former thought, that
in the unconscious things we find around us we are
dealing with an appearance, not with nature as it is.
That is a conscious existence, which to know fully
were to have that wider life and deeper consciousness for which our hearts cry out.   " To be one with
Nature " were not to lose our sense of life, but to have
it freed from the limitations which hedge it about
and make it teach us falsely ; it were to share in

living truth, the joyfulness, the passion, the repose, the rightness, which even now Nature images, though faintly and but afar off, to our hearts.

There is yet another respect in which it seems to me our thought of nature is inverted — naturally inverted owing to our partial apprehension, but in a way that corrects itself with growing knowledge. We think the organic world—that in which we discern the marks of life—the highest part of nature; it truly is the lowest. We have seen that, viewed by the eye of science, it is shown to be distinguished not by the addition of anything, but rather by an absence. It springs from the all-pervading order of nature by a limitation and confining of her powers.* Seen by the eye of the soul, it exhibits the same character. Organic life shows us the good powers of nature perverted to purposes that are not good. And thus our mingled feelings in respect to it receive an explanation. We admire, and cannot but admire, the order, the mutual subservience of all the parts and their interworking to common ends,

---

* See chapter vi. p. 143.

which the organic world displays. And thus, thinking that these characters of beauty and of order per-
tain exclusively to that region (where alone it is
visible to us), we have naturally concentrated our
admiration upon it, and have been almost forced to
think admirable also the ends which are thus sub-
served. We have been compelled to accept organic
life as excellent in its results and apparent objects, as
well as in its means; thinking the wonder and
beauty of those means were introduced for those
results alone! But how much more beautiful a
thought is open to us when we look on the organic
part of nature as, in these respects, but an exhibition
of the whole : and what relief it brings to the moral
constraint with which we have forced ourselves
to regard the universal rapine and utter selfhood
of the animal creation! Instead of possessing a
superadded and especial excellence of order and
adaptation, the organic world does but bring the
universal order and excellence of nature into our
little sphere of vision; there it is displayed on a
scale small enough for us to see, and we see it
beautiful. Forgetting this, we have extended to the

negative and evil elements, which are peculiar to the organic world (the subordination of everything to self-preservation and individual ends), the feelings which are appropriate only to that in it which is universal; we have carried on to the ends, the joyful admiration with which the means affect us— doing violence to our souls therein. Nature is beautiful, and in its organic applications we see its beauty; self-ends are evil, utterly and for ever, and in the organic world we see nature's beauty perverted to that evil.

Thus, there rightly arise in us the mingled feelings of delight and disgust, of admiration and of loathing, with which we look on the animal creation. Each of these feelings has its perfect justification, and its perfect place: the joy and admiration should embrace all nature; the loathing concentrate itself unchecked upon the purposes to which in the animal world nature is debased. An enemy hath done this: it is not life, this mere self-centred isolation; it is the mockery of it: an inverse, perverted life, laying its cruel bondage on our own souls too. But we hope for deliverance.

Animal existence shows us beautiful means perverted to evil ends: the glory of nature's order
yoked to the base car of selfish needs and graspings.
But it is not perverted thus unmarred; it could not
be. Even in mechanical adaptation the organic is the
weak part of nature; not as it seems to us, the strong
one. The glorious sweep of her order refuses to
revolve around that miserable centre of the self;
frailties, deformities, diseases, bear witness to the
strife, and testify the nobler sphere to which her
powers are vowed.

CHAPTER XII.

THE LIFE OF MAN.

BUT though organic life exhibits nature thus
bounded and tied down, its characters are not the
less rich in meaning. The laws which rule in it
are the universal laws, and speak the universal
language, exhibiting spiritual things to the eye of
sense. What other than a spiritual fact is this, the
most essential character of life: that it depends
upon the resistance or control of one form of force
by another? A passive force (properly called a
" passion"), kept in subjection, and only in regulated
and determined modes suffered to come into play;—
on this the seeming Life in Nature depends. Does
it not speak to us of that control of passion which is
Life indeed within us? Only by resistance, by

restraint, is Life. The passion on which it rests, uncontrolled, leads to corruption, ends in death.

We cannot but be struck with this fact in the history of the seed: opening the eyes of our souls to read it. Operated upon by the forces which bring its latent "passion" into play—the chemical affinities which its elements contain—the seed begins to undergo a change, the decomposition of its substance. But mark the difference. This change arises alike in the fertile and the infertile seed; it is the starting point at once of life and death. Resisted by the germ, it becomes the source of living action; it is the very power of growth; the chemical change, controlled, constitutes the life, and forms the basis of all the subsequent development: if unresisted, the seed decays; it sinks into corruption and is lost. Passion resisted is the source of life. Can we fail to hear in this a voice which addresses itself to our manhood? or to recognize a spiritual fact—a fact which our hearts alone can know— veiling itself behind these seeming laws of force?

Throughout all life it is so. The one fact of the control of passion is presented to us in all its forms.

The law of *tension,* translated out of the passive phenomenal terms into language that our souls can recognize is this:—it signifies holiness, rightness, self-control: it is our own Life portrayed before our eyes. The spiritual is made to " appear " to us, it is brought before our very senses, in these phenomenal laws of force, in which it is not, and yet is.

Again, how well we see herein how man differs from nature: what his fatal prerogative is. In nature passion is controlled; in man the control is wanting. Where nature rules and lives, man is a slave and dies. His passions (which duly subjugated are the very source and secret of his life), running riot without check, work in him mere corruption, and consume his manhood. Placed side by side, we see again, Life in Nature, Death in Man; a " law of death, working in his members."

And let us note again, how the evil of our present state is not our being in an evil place. This world which we call nature is not evil, it is the very appearance of the spiritual, of the highest and most perfect life. It is most right to appear; but our evil case is that we are feeling it to be not an appearance,

but the very truth. It is this makes the good evil
to us, and the very image of love to be a bondage
and a snare; makes us cry out on death, where only
life is to be found. We see how evil it would
be for us to feel the visual appearances of things
as if they were the reality, and to be acting so.
They would lead us into error, failure, sore per-
plexity; we should cry out to be delivered from
them, from a source of evil so pressing and so
constant! And yet how right and good it is that
these visual appearances should be. How well it is
for us to perceive them, knowing and feeling them to
be what they are; to see them, and yet not act,
nor find it possible to act, according to them.

It is thus with Nature too. Perfect our being,
and make us know it as it is, and it is no more
evil, nor the source of evil to us: it could no more
tempt or deceive; felt as appearing only, the appearance loses its perverting power; no more should we
do, or find it possible to do, the things which now
it is so hard for the best of us to avoid.

And again, seeing the relations which force bears
in the organic world, we have a key by which to

interpret it, wherever it extends, and in all its applications. The resistance to force in the living tissues, is *nutrition;* the liberation of that force effects a *function;* the former exists for, and is the condition of, the latter. Nutrition and function—organization and end—these are ideas which life associates with the operations of force, and they belong to it simply as force. It has no special endowment or prerogatives in the organic world; it presents simply its universal characters; and presents them there to our eye most truly. These ideas of nutrition and function are not of special, but of universal scope. All storing up of force is a nutrition; all liberation of it is the effecting of a function. To see the world as it is, we must carry this picture in our eye; to feel it rightly, our hearts must cast all things into this mould. For it is not in the material alone that this law has its place. It extends as widely, and soars as high as Life; it is the key above all to our own. All strife and failure, all subjection, baffling, wrong;—these are nutrition, they are the instruments of Life, the prophecies of its perfect ends. They store up the power, they make

14

the organization; and where these are, the function shall not fail. Life is in that which we call failure, which we feel as loss, which throws us back upon ourselves in anguish, which crushes us with despair: it is in aspirations baffled, hopes destroyed, efforts that win no goal. It is in the cross taken up. The silent flowers, the lilies of the field, teach us this lesson too. Nature takes up her cross; loses her life to gain it.

Thus Nature, which is so full of undefined, yet mighty spiritual significance, while it is yet not understood; which impresses our senses, and our hearts through them, with dim foreshadowings and glimmerings of the holiest things;—Nature, which is thus vaguely spiritual to our sensuous feeling, and which for that reason appeals to us so strongly through it, and is so dear to us;—which the poet sees flowing with springs of living water through every pore, yet half suspects them to be but the mirage of his own longing eye—seen according to the strict laws of science, is richer still with spiritual meaning. The indistinct and half-doubting emotion of delight and awe expands

itself into the clear apprehension of a spiritual order,
and rises into an infinite and confiding joy. Rooted
in a new and richer soil, the tree of our delight
spreads out its branches in a sunnier air.   It
is no longer our mere impression, still less our
mere fancy, to which Nature speaks of holiness,
of peace, of joy, of sacrifice, of that which we
most long to find in it; it speaks of these things
to our whole being.   Every faculty finds rest and
satisfaction in it.   It is no more one thing to our
heart and another to our thought; it is wholly one;
the best and highest appearing to us, as to us in our
lowliness it can appear; claiming to be known and
understood, as by the best and highest in us, alone,
it can be understood.

The reducing all events in nature to the mere
play of forces, brings, in the end, this lesson; our
souls, which it threatened to starve, it fills with a
higher life.

But we naturally ask further—If the physical be
the appearance of the spiritual world, how can we
connect the one with the other in our thoughts?
How shall we look through the apparent to the

actual, and give to each object or event among these things which we feel as real, its true relations? What, for instance, is the spiritual object presented to us by a tree, what by a rock, or house, or article of ordinary use?

In order to deal rightly with this question, neither lightly dismissing it as absurd, nor attempting vainly to give it a premature reply, we must recognize some other facts respecting Nature and our own relation to it. Especially we must remember, that in order to discern this relation, we must look, so to speak, along the line of physical events, and not across it. Each material object, as it arises in succession, is a new form or presentation to us of the same essential existence that was before; itself will pass away, and another form of that same existence will take its place. That existence, therefore, is not to be identified with individual things (which are but differing forms of the same), but is that which the whole succession represents. Thus, to take an instance, our question is not, What spiritual existence is perceived by us under the form of a tree? but, What presents itself under all the series of objects of which that tree is one? What is it that appears to us under the form of seed, of soil, of air, then of the organization of a tree, then, it may be, of ashes, flame, and smoke, and so on; both before and after, in an indefinite succession?' It is one existence that is presented to us throughout all, just as one solid may be presented to the eye under many different points of view. In seeking to learn the actual from the phenomenal, we must remember this, and frame our thoughts accordingly. What one existence makes us perceive in ways so manifold?

How far it is possible at present to advance, or whether it be possible to advance at all in this inquiry, we need not here decide. But one interesting question presents itself upon the threshold of it, a consideration of which may tend to make our path more clear.

Nothing in nature changes but the appearance; it is the varied representation to us of an existence which is ever the same. These changes of appearance, therefore—that is, the entire succession of change known as the " course of nature"—might be perceived by us through either of two causes: either a change apart from us, presenting the same existence differently: or a change affecting ourselves, and placing us in different relations to that existence.

It is our nature that by changes of our own condition we are made to feel as if other changes were occurring before us. In those dioramas, for example, in which the picture is fixed and the spectators are carried round, the impression upon them is precisely the same as if the scene moved before their eyes: nor is it possible for them to obtain any other. In a similar way, we are conscious of perceiving a succession of light and darkness—of day and night—while there is truly no such succession. There is a space illuminated by the sun's rays, and a shadow cast by the earth: our succession of day and night is but our being carried alternately from one into the other. In this case all men receive the same impression of external sequence from a change which affects them all.

It is clear, therefore, that a change affecting all men in common would perfectly account for the fact of their perceiving the changes that are perceived in nature. It would account also for their natural persuasion of the existence of these changes as external.

And there are reasons which command us to take this view. The fact that the "course of nature" consists in changes of form or appearance only, and involves nothing deeper there, is itself no inconsiderable evidence. For this is a result which a change affecting man would necessarily produce upon his consciousness. It is so, indeed, that we are ever made conscious of changes in ourselves. Therefore, it might be urged, since man is himself the subject of change, and the changes of appearance which we term the course of nature are of the kind which change in him would account for his perceiving, and since no other such effect of the change to which he is subject is apparent, his perception of the course of nature should be referred to this cause. It is the simplest view; it involves the least assumption; and claims on that ground to be received.

But there is other evidence. Some is derived

from the nature of *force*. If this be only felt by us, and do not exist in nature, it is a strong proof that the change with which we connect it is also in ourselves. To deny force in Nature, and leave there the change with which we feel it to be connected, seems not possible. To claim force as seated in our own feeling, implies that the change is also in ourselves; that we are altered, and not Nature, in her shifting phenomena.

So the feeling of force would be associated with change in man. We feel ourselves, when exerting it, changing that which is without us; but it is truly humanity that we affect. We can picture the idea to ourselves by the aid of a familiar illustration. A rower on a stream exerts his strength upon his oar, and perceives the shore as if it moved!—and not he only, but all who may be with him in the boat. The exertion of his force, affecting their common condition, presents to their perception a common change in the things around.

In the view we thus take many advantages are found. Our thought of nature is at once simplified and elevated. Instead of feeling ourselves to be a fixed centre, before which a mechanical universe marches with dead footsteps, we rise to the conception of a larger and sublimer universe, of worthier ends and grander sweep, upon the tide of which our little lives——nay, man's own larger life is borne; the true order and course of which includes the changing consciousness of man, painting so upon eternity for him a visionary time; which has for one of its least elements the pulsing of his heart and throbbing of his brain, which is enriched with all his passion, and bears his life-blood as a drop in its warm bosom; all being faintly imaged to his unperceiving eyes in changing garniture of earth and sky, from year to year.

Thus we do not seek any longer to attach our marvellous consciousness to these passive things which seem, but cannot be, its causes. It has a worthier, a more reasonable source. These material things (which are found to be mere " phenomena ") and their changes (in which there is no change) are not the causes of that which we experience; they are the appearances which a deeper cause, unseen, brings up before us. They are projected from our eye, and have another lesson for us than that which we read upon their surface. Surpassing them as they surpass a dream, stands the true universe which they reveal.

And not only is our thought of Nature raised and made clearer by accepting a change in man as the cause of our perception of external change; a new proof is given us of the unity of men. For not only is the change which affects us common to all, and the same in respect to all, but the action of any one of us is shown to influence the race; because all men perceive, or may perceive, the effects of the actions of all others. Since the action of any one man changes, really or possibly, the consciousness of all—as when one man moves any-thing, all around perceive it moved—it follows (upon the supposition that has been made) that all are united with all others—though they may be un-conscious of the tie—and partake in that which each one does and is. It must be so, if the effects of our actions are truly wrought within and not without. Humanity is proved one by all the evidence which goes to establish that the seeming changes perceived

around are signs of a true change that takes place
in ourselves.

And these two thoughts conduct us to a result
in which, while we press forward towards farther
light, we may yet rest with present satisfaction.
If man is one, and if some spiritual work pertaining
to humanity, and embracing, therefore, every member of it, be the true cause of all that we experience,
then our hearts, at least, may be at rest. The
universal Life bears man's destiny within it; and
not the meanest labour, the most trivial accident,
fails of contributing its part. If, as we have seen,
to understand our life, we must look beyond the
seeming, we see here the guide by which we may
interpret it. The carrying out of a change in man,
this is the meaning of it; this the unseen fact.
It is not wasted as it seems.

And yet once more our hearts turn to Nature
as their guide. What is it that is imaged there?
What fact presents to our eyes this scene of mingled
life and death, of ruin and of order, and reveals to
our more humble and instructed gaze life springing
out of death, ruling decay, embracing ruin as its

instrument? What is it shows us *becoming* as its constant law; the loss of each thing for the being of each other; all giving itself for all; life dying that other life may be; dying, but in that very death most truly living?

What fact is imaged here? What is the keynote of this mingled harmony? Do we not hear it in one word—Redemption? Of death, and life raised up from death; of life bestowed by death, and perfected through it; of sacrifice, which is the law of being and the root of joy; of these things Nature speaks to us. She points us to her Maker, in Him who gave His Son.

CHAPTER XIII.

CONCLUSION.

IT may probably be felt by those to whom the ideas
on which I have thus briefly dwelt are presented for
the first time, that what I have said amounts merely
to suggestion, and that of a doubtful character. I
may say, therefore, that I have designed my remarks merely as suggestions; and have sought only
to present an outline of certain methods of regarding the great problems of our life, which seem to
me to possess a good foundation, and to promise
results of a different character from those which the
methods hitherto in use have yielded, at least in
recent times. To suggest, ever so imperfectly, ideas
of this order, if they should be found to have a real
value, seems to me a task worthy of my highest
efforts. Nor do I believe that they will be entirely

in vain ; because the ideas themselves seem to me to be not the hasty speculations of any individual, but the legitimate fruit of time.   In so far as they are true, they are a boon which our dead fathers have won for us—the inheritance with which they have enriched us.

Can we believe that the long inquiries of men into the facts and laws that are presented to their senses should fail to give them an increased power of dealing with other facts and laws, of which not the senses but the heart and soul take cognizance? Or can we believe that any other result should ensue from this increased power than that the demands of man's moral nature should be proved true, also, to his intellect?

I am myself convinced that the chief obstacle, now, to our advance in this path is the conviction that it is closed to us :—a conviction natural enough, indeed, through repeated failures, yet by those very failures proved untrue.   If in this volume I have done anything to shake this conviction in any mind, and to induce the feeling that it may be premature and presumptuous, I have done enough.   That little, or even nothing, is completed in it, I shall hold a light reproof. How should that present finished results which waits even now for its beginning? A field ripe for the harvest does not yield loaves of bread.

We are in some degree sensible of the presumption which may be involved in bold speculations and large expectations of knowledge; but we think little of the presumption that is involved in denials and in the assumption that we can mark out limits. Our pride may pass if it will but wrap itself in the cloak of humility. Yet I venture to say, that no presumption of extravagant affirmation that has shamed the past, equals in presumptuous arrogance those bold negations and prophetic mappings out of man's capacities, for which our own age will have to blush. Nor does it affect this question, that the men who have propounded these invertedly ambitious doctrines have acted under the influence of the best motives, and have been men of an eminent modesty. Private conceit is seldom an accompaniment of eminent ability; nor is there any reason to believe that the most audacious speculators of former times have been wanting in personal modesty, while their aims have been unquestionably good. Happily, the human destiny is ruled by higher powers than the personal characters of men; nor could it be otherwise than that, in its aspiring vanity, the mind of man should swing from the positive to the negative side—from absurd assurance of knowledge to absurder assurance of inability to know—before it finally assumed its true level, in a hopeful, laborious, and confiding patience.

When that time comes, I think it will be seen that the real difficulty we have encountered—the real source of the despair which has seized so many of our chief thinkers, and has made them (against all their best native instincts and acquired tendencies) presume to limit the possible advance of man, even though they thus debarred him precisely from those gifts which are of highest value—has been our not expecting enough. We have failed because we had cast our reckoning of God's bounty too low—as, indeed, how could we do otherwise? We have despaired because we could not believe in, nor receive, a gift so rich as He has given us.

A little petty perfecting of knowledge, such as we have aspired after, we shall never have; they tell us most truly who tell us so. God forbid we should —forbid that His givings should be limited by our desires; His bountiful surprises by our anticipations. But, darkened by our own expectations, and seeing nothing but their failure, we do not see that they fail only because a success altogether beyond any possible expectations is placed in our hands; nay, that in this very failure that greater and better success consists.

We may see this greater success involved in our seeming failure in two ways:—

First. If we find that all our attempts to fathom existence by thought are in vain, and that we can only arrive at conceptions which cannot be the truth because they involve contradictions; then how can we fail to see the different attitude in which our emotions and our moral feelings are placed in regard to our belief? If that which we can conceive cannot be true, then why may not our moral powers be, in respect to truth, the guide and judge? The idea, which naturally arises when the short-coming of the

15

intellect is realized, that we have no power of knowing, is based only on forgetfulness of the fact that we have powers which mere intellect does not include, and to which the intellect may be made the servant. If our thoughts have not authority, our hearts may be made judges. This is given to us in the seeming denial of our power to know. We may translate all that the intellect can apprehend into moral terms; may read in it a spiritual significance; may affirm *that*—duly fulfilling the conditions of the case—to be the truth. From that which the heart knows we have to trace, as an appearance, that which the intellect and the sense perceive. Some little attempt towards this I have made in the foregoing pages.

Or, secondly, we may think thus: suppose, instead of seeking to penetrate the nature of things, men had been trying to discover whether *man* was in a normal or a defective state; had been seeking to discover this as a necessary preliminary to the solution of ulterior problems. Then would not the discovery which now seems like a fatal bar to knowledge—the discovery, namely, that our perception and feeling are not true; that we naturally and universally apply the idea of existence falsely, and only by long effort learn that what we take for existence is but phenomenal—would not this discovery have been hailed as the very answer that was sought, and as a step of most hopeful augury? This means that man is in a diseased, a wanting state.* It is the starting-point of inquiry, not the end. It seems like the end only because we have not been asking the right question. We have been seeking wrongly, but God has answered us aright.

For it is wonderful to see what a new light arises, and what doors open, when we take as a guide to our thoughts this idea of a false feeling, arising from a wanting state, in man. It is, in one aspect, one of the least results, though in another it is the sum of all, that our whole thought, our very science, is made Christian.

Inconceivable things are given us through this knowledge respecting man, which comes to us in the deceptive guise of an inability on his part to know. It were not possible to have believed that so much

---

* See Chapter IX., p. 183.

was in store for us. I know no question that the
intellect desires to pierce, or the heart in its secret
chambers weeps over or tries to forget, which does
not stand in a fresh light before it, and bend itself to
give it confirmation. Unwittingly to ourselves, God
has kept us in the right path, He has made us do
what we had no thought of doing.

Do not *we* deal so with our children?

APPENDIX.

AN ATTEMPT TOWARDS A MORE EXTENDED INDUCTION OF THE LAWS OF LIFE.

[The following is the Essay referred to in the Introduction and at page 53.]

THE motion of a pendulum consists of two portions —a downward movement caused by gravitation, and an upward movement, theoretically equal in amount, which is produced by the momentum arising from the former. The essential condition of the sequence of the upward movement is that the downward movement should be resisted in a definite manner. The gravitating motion, not being completed, becomes a motion opposed to gravity.

The molecular changes recognized in living bodies are of two kinds — those which result in that arrangement of the particles which constitutes organic matter, and those which tend to reduce organic matter to the condition of inorganic compounds. The former of these motions (or forms of action) is known as nutrition, the latter as decomposition.

It is sometimes said that decomposition results from the operation of chemical affinity, and that nutrition is the operation of the vital force. I shall for the present use these words with these meanings. If the idea of a resistance to the motion of decomposition be introduced, it may readily be conceived that the chemical and vital actions (as above defined) bear to each other the same relation as that which exists between the downward and upward motions of a pendulum. The chemical motion, not being completed, may become a motion opposed to chemical attraction.

The proofs I shall adduce of this hypothesis are—

I. That it is indicated by the phenomena of life.

II. That it is conformable to the general course of nature.

I. It is indicated by the phenomena of life.

I do not now speak of the origination of life.

As, in treating of the motions of a pendulum, the existence of the pendulum and its first upward movement are assumed, so I assume for my present purpose the existence of organized bodies, and therein of that organic arrangement of particles which I affirm to be thereafter renewed and increased through the medium of chemical action.

Nor do I now speak of the forms assumed by living substances, or that which is properly termed Organisation. The following remarks relate to the primary fact of life, the production of organic matter.

And further, I do not design to attempt a complete explanation of the facts to be adduced. I consider them in that relation only, in which they may serve to indicate the chain that connects vital action with the material changes which directly and causally precede it.

In the vegetable world, the dependence of vital action upon an incomplete or resisted process of chemical change is indicated by such facts as these.

The fertilized seed grows as it decays.

The chemical process of fermentation maintains the growth of vegetable organisms.

Organic matter, of whatever kind, spontaneously decaying in the presence of the atmosphere, seldom fails to be covered with fungi and other plants of a low type.

The ordinary growth of plants has been shown by Müller to be intimately connected with chemical or decomposing changes occurring in the soil.

The decomposition of carbonic acid and production of organic matter by the leaves of plants has been shown, by Dr. Draper, to involve a decomposition effected in the leaf by light.

In each of these instances the vital action appears to be the secondary process. The infertile seed decays in the same manner as the fruitful one. Fermentation may take place without any development of the yeast plant, although less rapidly. Ordinary putrefaction and decomposition of the soil are not necessarily dependent upon the development of living structures.

In the phenomena of animal life a similar relation of vital to chemical action may be traced.

The egg in the act of development absorbs oxygen, and undergoes also, in part, a decomposing change.

Vegetable infusions, while decaying, swarm with animalculæ; and putrefying animal bodies are thronged with forms of life.

In the act of digestion, the first stage is one of decompositon of the food.

Blood is arterialized by the union of oxygen with a part of its constituents.

In one form of the multiplication of cells, a parent cell decays while others are developed within it.

In the successive formation of hairs, the new hair, as described by Mr. Paget, appears to be developed as an offshoot from its decaying predecessor.

Functional activity, which ever involves a disintegrating change, is a cause of increased energy of the nutritive process.

The decomposing changes which constitute secretion, as in the liver for example, appear to institute an increased development of the vital condition of the blood.

I have enumerated these simple and well-known facts with a view of indicating the broad basis upon which the general idea of the direct dependence of vital on chemical processes reposes.

If they be more closely regarded, the conception which they convey to the mind, either singly or together, becomes more distinct. The chemical affinities of the elements of organized bodies are common to them with all other forms of matter, and constitute, therefore, a legitimate starting-point. These affinities, the conditions being suitable, give rise to a molecular motion which has been aptly termed downward, and which, if it continue, ends in the production of the simplest compounds. But if this movement be resisted or interrupted in its course, there will exist, as it were, a momentum of motion, which must take another direction, or exist in another form. Now, a molecular motion of chemical character, but in a direction different from that of the chemical attraction, constitutes the very definition of vital action, or of life. It is an upward molecular motion in relation to decomposition as a downward one. The decomposition and the life, taken together, resemble, as before suggested, the movement of a pendulum. They make up a true vibration.

Whatsoever may be the exact nature of that

attraction which is termed chemical affinity, there can be little doubt that it includes as one element a tendency to the approximation of certain particles. It is in one aspect, probably in its primary aspect, an approximating force. In this respect it presents an analogy to the force of gravitation, which it can hardly lead us into error fully to recognize, and on which, indeed, the illustration of the pendulum is based.

If we now endeavour to carry the conception of the vital process more into detail, the view which has been taken of it affords an easy clue.

In the act of chemical change certain particles of matter are approaching each other, moved thereto by mutual attracting influences. If it be conceived that from some cause (not as yet defined) the perfect approximation of such particles is prevented, what so naturally ensues as that they pass by and go beyond each other, the very impulse of their attraction becoming thus the source of their separation ?

What else have we in life? Is not the living body constituted by certain particles of matter en-

dowed with approximating tendencies, yet carried
perpetually into divergent relations?

Again: Particles of matter carried by an approximating force thus into a state of divergence tend
perpetually to renew the approximating motion.
The divergent state is in itself entirely unstable.
The upward motion of a pendulum is the type of
it—a state of ever-changing action, which no sooner
attains its maximum than it begins straightway to
decline. Is it not so with life?

Upon the view thus presented, it is easy to conceive of life as a state of action contrary to chemical
affinity, but constantly maintained by the operation
of chemical attractions. It is not less easy to understand how the vital action thus arising should be
increased or intensified beyond such an amount, or
such an energy, as would be proportionate to the
original chemical affinities from which it springs.
The downward motion of a pendulum becomes an
equal upward movement, the loss of motion from
friction and the resistance of the air being allowed
for; but if this downward motion be accelerated or
increased by any other force acting, or capable of

acting, in the same direction, the upward movement is proportionately greater.   Thus the vital action which ensues from any given chemical change may have added to it, as it were, the momentum of whatever forces can add their impetus to the molecular movement which constitutes the chemical change.

How much of heat, or light, or electricity comes thus to assume the form of vital action, may perhaps be estimated by the amount of the absorption of those forces which may be found to accompany the vital processes.

But to embrace all the phenomena contained in even the simplest idea of life, regarding it, that is, as the mere bringing into existence of organic matter, it is necessary to extend somewhat the conception I have suggested.   In the vibration of a pendulum the same portion of matter falls, and rises again by virtue of its fall.   But a falling body may impart its momentum, and, not rising itself, may cause in other matter a proportionate upward movement.   The requisite mechanism is simple, and involves only the one condition, that the body receiving the impulse shall move most easily in the desired direction; that is, its motion in other directions must be resisted, or resisted *more*. The postulate is, as before, *a definite resistance.*

The same thing is presented to us, in a still simpler form, in the transference of heat from one body to another; the one becoming warm as the other cools, and in consequence of such cooling, or in the action of an ordinary balance, of which the one arm, by its fall, causes the rise of the other.

These few conceptions, gathered from familiar facts, give us, to a certain extent, a perfect grasp of some of the most baffling phenomena of life.

As one example, let us take the germination of the seed. Put into conditions which elicit, or permit, the operation of the chemical affinities it begins to decompose. The downward, or approximative, motion thus arising, imparted to other elements in the seed, which are so constructed as to admit of motion most readily in the opposite or vital direction, becomes in those elements a motion of life, or growth.

One fact connected with the germination of the seed deserves especial notice, namely, that it is attended with an increase of temperature. The growth cannot, therefore, result from a conversion of heat into any other form of force. The true idea would seem to be, that there is, as it were, an excess of chemical action above that which becomes the vital action; and which excess, therefore, assumes the ordinary form of heat. A falling body, if it impart its entire momentum of motion to another, produces no heat; but if only some of the motion be imparted, a proportionate amount of heat is manifested.

As another instance, we may take together the growth of mould on decaying matter, and the process of digestive assimilation. The forces at work, and the mode of their operation, appear, in both these cases, to be the same as those which we have traced in germination. The chemical motion of certain particles becomes the vital motion of certain other particles, which present to it an appropriate resistance. The vegetable germs which develop into the mouldy growth, represent accurately enough the living cells, or other organisms, with which the decomposing food is brought in contact.

The oxidation of the blood presents the same idea to us perhaps in its simplest form. Certain particles of the venous blood enter into union with the oxygen of the atmosphere, with formation of carbonic acid: a manifest process of decomposition. But another part of the same blood, which resists this decomposing action, or refuses to undergo it, receives therefrom an impulse which causes its higher vitalization and fits it to be the agent in nutrition. Is there in this process, regarded in its general outline, and apart from theory, anything more hard of comprehension than the coincident fall and rise of the respective arms of a balance?

In the same light, also, may be viewed the higher vitalization of the blood effected by its partial decomposition in the secreting glands. And with these may be classed the excretive or other decomposing changes which so generally accompany the process of metamorphosis. The silkworm spins its cocoon by a decomposition or retrograde chemical action, which imparts to the remaining blood a higher vital status fitted for the more elevated grade on which it is about to enter.

The process of digestion, however, presents other points which claim remark.

In the first place, those substances only which are undergoing, or tending to chemical change, will serve as food. The food supplies not only the materials for nutrition, and for the production of heat, but, in the form of its decomposing action, the *life* of the being which consumes it. Without the chemical action in the food, no amount of materials and of heat avails for nutrition.

Plants live upon carbonic acid and ammonia; but, as stated by Müller, carbonate of ammonia, in every form, is a poison to them.

2ndly. The various kinds of food produce various forms of vital action, quite independently of the materials of which they consist. The food of all animals scarcely varies in its elements. But in the nature and intensity of the chemical changes it undergoes, it presents innumerable and most important variations. And upon these, as one element, the characteristic differences of vital action

16

in the various tribes of animals, doubtless, in part depend.

Nothing can more strikingly confirm this view than the difference of the vegetable structures which respectively accompany the vinous and acetous fermentations. Special modes of chemical action will alone maintain specific forms of life.

3rdly. The vitalization of the elements of the food is effected, not through the medium of its spontaneous decomposition, but by more energetic chemical changes wrought by the digestive fluids. The vital motion is conditional upon a decomposing motion intensified by contact with the products of secretion.

Parallel instances are not wanting. Muscles waste unless their decomposition be rendered more rapid by those influences which bring them into functional activity. Plants attain no vigour unless decomposition be hastened in their leaves by light. And the earliest changes in the embryo, " consisting in the formation of a membrane upon the exterior, while a large part of the included substance undergoes liquefaction," indicate the operation of the same law. The phenomena of inflammation fall into the same category. Two things are evident in it:—first, an abnormal activity of the chemical or decomposing processes; and, secondly, an increased vital action consequent thereupon.

Into these two groups the events which constitute inflammation plainly resolve themselves. Its causes are ever such as either directly carry decomposition to an excess, or have practically the same effect by arresting vital action. Its tendency is primarily to disintegration, or the death of parts. It is in its beginning an increased chemical or anti-vital change.

In this derangement of the actions which constitute life consists that unseen change which precedes and causes the various physical and mechanical phenomena which observation recognizes or the microscope reveals. And closely following this accelerated decomposition, comes, by the law of life, that increased vital action upon which a prevalent idea of inflammation has been based.

Thus the conception of chemical and vital action as constituting a vibration is found to unfold particular phenomena of life. But it does more than

16—2

this. It shows why in the actual life of the animal these two forms of action constitute an inseparable chain, and, when regarded as unconnected processes, an inextricable maze. That which should be on this supposition, is precisely that which is; vital action perpetually followed by chemical, and chemical again by vital. From first to last, that is the history of life.

The varieties of vital action also, the differences between specific kinds of life, find a satisfactory origin in the scarcely less numerous varieties of chemical action. The supposition of specific vital properties or tendencies falls by the abstraction of its foundation. The varieties of life are the varieties of chemical action presented under another aspect.

The elements, therefore, which are involved in this lowest idea of life are two—a chemical attraction or force, and a definite resistance to that force. From these two elements result chemical and vital action. But there is rightly speaking no vital force. The action of a pendulum involves the same ideas—a gravitating attraction or force, and a definite resistance; resulting in a gravitating and an ascending action. But there is in the pendulum no " *ascending force.*"

II. This view of vital action is conformable to the general course of nature. The entire succession of events, which we call the course of nature, involves essentially the same elements as those which we have found in life, namely, an action and a resistance. A force, or form of action, resisted, assumes of necessity another direction or another form. This is the law, the results of which have been grouped under the denomination of the correlation or conversion of the forces. That motion takes the direction of least resistance, in one aspect of the case, embraces the whole. It is not difficult to trace the working of this law so far as our knowledge is exact and definite. It becomes obscure precisely where our ideas lose their distinctness.

Motion, if it be resisted, becomes heat or light, or some other force, but only on condition that it *be* resisted. Heat, if its transmission or continuance be resisted, assumes other forms; thus it passes freely through a homogeneous metal and undergoes no change, but if forcibly applied to a non-conductor, as glass, that is, to a body which resists it, it is changed into motion, evidenced by the fracture of the glass; or at the point of junction of two metals, where its passage is resisted, it becomes electricity. Electricity again passes almost without change along a wire, until its quantity becomes too great for the wire to convey, when that which is resisted assumes the form of heat or light. The electric spark arises only at those points at which the passage of the current is resisted.

The production of electricity from chemical action may be traced to the same law.

If the flame of an ordinary taper be observed, a current of wax is seen rising towards the flame. There exists also another invisible current, viz. that of the air towards the same flame, but in the opposite direction. The atmosphere, however, being a compound body, this atmospheric current is necessarily double, the nitrogen being repelled from the flame as the oxygen approaches it.

Conceive now a flame supported by hydrogen on the one side and air upon the other. On the one hand the hydrogen being attracted to the point of chemical action constitutes a single current in that direction; the oxygen being also attracted, there arises in the air a double current, one towards and one away from the flame. Now the hydrogen current towards the flame and the nitrogen current from the flame being on opposite sides are in the same direction; and it may be conceived, in theory at least, that by a mechanical arrangement of tubes these two currents might be united, so that the impulse of the current of nitrogen *from* the flame should serve to augment the momentum of the hydrogen current *towards* the flame, facilitating by so much its union with the oxygen.

In a zinc and platinum galvanic battery the process which takes place is the same—the element added is a resistance to the freely circulating currents we have been considering. For the particles of the zinc are attracted to the point of chemical union in the same way as those of hydrogen are attracted, but the cohesion of its structure resists their motion. Hence there is produced in it a tension, which, while on the one hand it represents the motion of its particles towards the acid, *resisted*, constitutes, on the other, the electric state.

But the dilute acid being a compound body, there exists in it, as before noted in the atmosphere, a double current; the oxygen moving towards, the hydrogen away from, the point of chemical union. The impulse of the hydrogen being imparted to the particles of the platinum, and the motion resisted in the latter by its cohesion of structure, there is produced in it, as in the zinc plate, a state of electric tension, but in a direction away from the point of chemical action. These two tensions, therefore, are really in one direction: unite them by a conductor of that special form of motion, and what ensues but a current, adding the momentum of the tension of the platinum to that of the zinc, and facilitating by so much the union of the zinc with the oxygen?

This view of the production of galvanism by chemical action receives strong confirmation from the state of tension generated in portions of gold by hydrochloric and nitric acid, separated by a porous partition. From what cause can such tension arise but from the attraction of the chlorine resisted by

the cohesion of the gold, and how can the completion of the circuit avail to determine chemical
action, if it be not by overcoming that cohesion,
through the union of the two momenta?

Other instances of the law that change of one
form of action into another is caused by a resistance
to the action so changed, I need not now adduce.
It is, indeed, sufficient to inquire to what else can
such a change be referred? or to what else but
to an incredible multiplication of specific properties,
before which even the imagination stands aghast?

This, then, we find in Nature :—Motion assuming
endless forms in accordance with an ever-varying
resistance.   But the resistance, though ever-varying,
is one.   To one force, indeed, there can be but one
resistance: if force be single, although multiform,
resistance, although multiform, must be single also.

Force being regarded as motion, all the modes
and forms of resistance might be generalized under
the idea of *cohesion;* the variety in it depending
upon diversity of structure or arrangement.

If a ball strike against a wall, its motion, to a
certain extent, ceases and is changed.   But the

resistance of the wall is no property of the matter of which it is composed; if the cohesion of the particles forming it be destroyed, it no longer resists or converts the motion. In the same matter, friction produces heat or electricity, according to most inconsiderable diversities of structure. Light is partially resisted and converted into heat, if the surface of glass be roughened. All non-conductors or resisting bodies are such by virtue of their structure: not the elements, but the mode in which they are arranged determines their resisting power. A gaseous mixture of oxygen, hydrogen, nitrogen, and carbonic acid, resists the electric current, but the same elements united into a muscle conduct it readily.

The resistance to chemical action, which causes it to become vital action, might be termed *organic cohesion.*

A comparison of organic cohesion with the cohesion of inorganic bodies, which, by resistance, changes one form of force into another, elicits many points of resemblance.

For example, the change of the force depends upon a certain relation between the force and the resistance. An excess of force overcomes the cohesion, and destroys thereby the power of resistance. Too hard a blow breaks a solid body: an excess of electricity rends a non-conductor. So, too intense a chemical action destroys vitality. May not putrefying matters and some poisons act in this way?

Again: the resistance remaining the same, a given motion produces entirely different results, according to its amount or intensity. Thus, if a bullet be projected against an open door with very little force, its motion is stopped, a certain amount of heat is generated, but the door remains unmoved: if it be fired from a pistol, it passes through the door, which still remains unmoved; but if it be projected with an intermediate degree of force, the door is moved upon its hinges. Much that is similar to this takes place in the living body.

The mere passive decay of a tissue designed for use produces no vital action; an unused muscle wastes; excessive or morbid decomposition may equally fail to be followed by the nutritive process, as when death ensues from prolonged over-exertion, or atrophy from inflammation. Only an intermediate intensity of chemical action, not varying much from that which attends the normal activity of the tissues, will maintain the vital process.

There are some facts which, upon a cursory view, might give the impression that the growth of living organisms is the cause rather than the effect of chemical action or decomposition. The production of fermentation by yeast is an example.

The true meaning of these facts appears at once upon a reference to the inorganic world.

The completion of the circuit in a galvanic battery may occasion, and always increases, the chemical action. When the uniting wire is small and becomes heated by the current, the chemical action takes place more freely in proportion to the readiness with which the heat of the wire can be dissipated. Or, more simply, if two weights be suspended over a pulley, the more easily the one is made to ascend, the more readily and rapidly will the other descend.

The presence of living matter facilitates decay, by affording a ready passage, as it were, to the resulting action. Life bears the same relation to decomposition that the galvanic current bears to the union of oxygen with zinc, or that the ascent of one weight bears to the descent of another. Living germs permit decay by taking up—absorbing, it might almost be said—the resulting force. They act the part of a good conductor around the heated wire. I may observe here an instance of beneficent adapta-, tion. Decay being to so great an extent dependent upon the occurrence of vital action, the source of life is husbanded and reserved for the purposes of life. If complete decomposition took place rapidly in the soil independently of the existence of vegeta-tion, how sad a barrenness would overspread the earth. But God has ordained it otherwise, and the life-pro-ducing chemistry tarries at his bidding for the germ.

Motion takes the direction of least resistance. If the resistance be absolute this direction is at right angles to the line of the original motion. That this must be the case is obvious, the rectangular direction being the mean between the momentum of the motion and the resistance supposed. And it is so in fact. A current of air striking against a flat surface passes off at a right angle in all directions: a soft mass propelled against such a surface becomes flattened, that is, expands at right angles to the line of motion; and a solid body, under similar conditions, tends to the same result, as evidenced by the fracture it undergoes if the momentum be sufficient.

This law may perhaps be traced in the production of magnetism from electricity. For a wire, while it conducts, at the same time resists, the electric current, and the iron bar across which it passes presents to it (that is, to a certain proportion of it) a direction of less resistance, at the same time altering its form. But the resistance of the wire tends to turn the electric current at right angles, which is the direction it assumes when it becomes magnetism.

If the resistance be not absolute (that is, if the motion be only partially turned from its direction, or if, it being entirely turned, the original force continues in operation so that it is constantly renewed), the direction assumed will lie between the original course and a line at right angles to it.

And if the force producing the motion and the resistance are both of continued operation, the resulting motion will be curvilinear. One illustration will suffice. A bubble rising rapidly through water passes upwards either in one or many curves, and frequently in a spiral, closely resembling the form of a corkscrew.

So, also, a ball of moderate specific gravity, sinking in water, falls, not in a straight line, but in one or many curves, diverging more or less in proportion to the difference of density between itself and the medium through which it sinks. The curve described by the falling body represents the composition of two motions—namely, a downward movement turned at right angles, and a continuous gravitating movement.

That the motion of a body gravitating through a resisting medium will be turned at right angles, becomes obvious, when it is considered that the portion of the medium between the gravitating body and the point of attraction, is the densest and most resisting portion, both from the influence of the attracting mass upon the medium itself and from the pressure of the gravitating body.

There is one simple application of these principles, which I mention on account of its value as an illustration of the conception of life.

The motions of the heavenly bodies having been treated as if occurring in a vacuum, it has become necessary to assume a special impulse at right angles to the gravitating motion of the planets. But if the planets be conceived as gravitating from any requisite distance through a plenum or resisting medium, their motion towards the sun, being turned at right angles, the centrifugal force is no longer a hypothesis, but a demonstrable result.

Or the facts may be regarded from another point of view. Conceive a planet, at the aphelion, gravitating towards the sun, but under such a resistance that its motion assumes the actual curve of its orbit. Under these conditions it falls by virtue of its gravitation—not to the sun, but beyond it. When it reaches its perihelion, it will have attained a momentum of motion which would carry it through a precisely corresponding curve, in opposition now to gravity, to the aphelion again—the point from which it started. This is the motion of a pendulum starting from the zenith and returning to the zenith, but with its point of gravitation within, instead of external to, its circuit. But a planet thus oscillating around the sun, would have less than the actual velocity, and would be, at the aphelion, momentarily at rest.

Two elements have to be supplied to bring the hypothesis into accordance with the facts—first, the resistance which turns the gravitating motion into the elliptic form, and secondly, the velocity of the planet at the aphelion. Both of these are supplied by supposing the planet to have gravitated through a resisting medium from a greater distance. An ordinary kite raised above the earth by being drawn through the resisting atmosphere, sufficiently illustrates the principle upon which the argument is based.*

It is obvious that this hypothesis embraces also the motions of the double stars. Two masses, gravitating towards each other through a plenum, diverge as they approach, and falling beyond each other, continue in a mutual revolution which is in truth but a prolonged vibration.

---

* This illustration is suffered to remain, for illustration's sake; but I am aware that the best authorities deny that the velocity really possessed by the planets could be thus derived.

This motion of the double stars is the idea of life enacted on a different scale. Atoms, or stars, " endowed with approximating tendencies, carried perpetually into divergent relations !"

Thus, not only in the motions of the pendulum, but in those also of the stars, we might find an analogue of the essential process in organic life—a chemical force, resisted, producing a chemical and a vital motion.

THE END.

For EU product safety concerns, contact us at Calle de José Abascal, 56–1°, 28003 Madrid, Spain or eugpsr@cambridge.org.